The Quest of Treasure Island:

A Magical Journey to Wealth

Aura Marx

Introduction

Welcome to a journey that transcends the conventional boundaries of personal finance and self-improvement, weaving them into a cohesive narrative that speaks to the heart and mind alike. This book is an odyssey, exploring the intricate dance between the accumulation of wealth and the pursuit of personal growth. It is crafted for those who seek not just financial independence but a richer, more fulfilling life—a life adorned with purpose, driven by values, and enriched by experiences.

Within these pages lies a holistic approach to wealth, one that acknowledges the multifaceted nature of true prosperity. We embark on this voyage with the understanding that wealth extends beyond monetary gains to include the wealth of knowledge, relationships, experiences, and the legacy we aspire to leave behind. This book is an invitation to explore the symbiotic relationship between financial strategies and personal development, each reinforcing and elevating the other.

As we navigate through the chapters, we delve into the principles of strategic financial planning, mindful spending, and savvy investing, all while fostering personal virtues of resilience, adaptability, and ethical living. We examine the importance of aligning one's financial endeavors with deeper life goals and values, ensuring that the quest for wealth is a reflection of one's true self.

This book is not just a guide but a companion on your journey toward a life of abundance and personal actualization. It is for those who dare to dream, those ready to redefine success on their own terms, and those committed to building a legacy that transcends material wealth.

Contents

Chapter 1: The Map to Hidden Riches

Uncover your wealth mindset

Embarking on the journey to wealth often begins not with a step, but a shift—a profound transformation in the way one perceives and interacts with the concept of wealth itself. This transformative shift is what many refer to as uncovering one's wealth mindset. It's a pivotal moment that marks the transition from merely aspiring to financial security to actively cultivating it. The wealth mindset isn't just about harboring dreams of affluence; it's about nurturing a set of beliefs and attitudes that make the accumulation and sustainable growth of wealth possible.

At the core of the wealth mindset is the belief in abundance, contrasting sharply with the scarcity mindset that plagues many. While a scarcity mindset views wealth as a finite pie, where one person's gain is another's loss, the wealth mindset sees wealth as an expansive, boundless ocean, capable of growing and providing for all. This fundamental belief in abundance allows individuals to approach wealth creation with optimism, seeing opportunities where others see obstacles.

Another cornerstone of the wealth mindset is the emphasis on value creation. Individuals with a wealth mindset understand that wealth is not just earned—it's created through the provision of value to others. This perspective shifts the focus from competition to contribution, encouraging individuals to think about how they can solve problems, fulfill needs, and make life better for others. By focusing on value creation, individuals open themselves up to myriad opportunities for wealth generation that are both fulfilling and sustainable.

Self-efficacy plays a significant role in the wealth mindset. This refers to the belief in one's ability to achieve goals and overcome challenges. A strong sense of self-efficacy empowers individuals to set ambitious financial goals and persist in the face of setbacks. It's this resilience and confidence that differentiate those who merely dream of wealth from those who actively shape their financial destinies.

Education and continuous learning are also integral to the wealth mindset. The landscape of wealth creation is ever-changing, with new opportunities and challenges emerging with advancements in technology, shifts in the economy, and changes in consumer behavior. Those with a wealth mindset are committed to lifelong learning, constantly acquiring new skills, knowledge, and insights that enable them to navigate this dynamic terrain effectively.

Furthermore, the wealth mindset involves a strategic approach to risk. Contrary to popular belief, individuals with a wealth mindset are not reckless gamblers but calculated risk-takers. They understand that risk is an inherent part of wealth creation and that avoiding risk altogether is often the riskiest move. However, they approach risk with caution, conducting thorough research, seeking advice from mentors, and weighing the potential rewards against the risks. This balanced approach to risk allows them to seize opportunities without jeopardizing their financial stability.

Networking and mentorship are also pivotal in cultivating a wealth mindset. Wealth creation is seldom a solitary journey; it's a voyage that benefits immensely from the wisdom, experience, and support of others. By building a network of mentors, peers, and advisors, individuals can gain insights, learn from the successes and failures of others, and find encouragement and accountability. This communal aspect of the wealth mindset underscores the importance of relationships in achieving financial success.

In essence, uncovering your wealth mindset is about more than just adjusting your financial strategies; it's about transforming your entire approach to life and wealth. It's about shifting from a passive stance, where wealth is something that happens to you, to an active stance, where wealth is something, you consciously create. This mindset embraces the principles of abundance, value creation, self-efficacy, continuous learning, strategic risk-taking, and the power of community.

As individuals embark on this transformative journey, they'll find that the wealth mindset not only paves the way for financial prosperity but also fosters a life rich in purpose, growth, and fulfillment. It's a journey that begins with a shift in perspective, one that opens the door to endless possibilities and empowers individuals to shape their financial destinies.

Deciphering the Clues of Financial Freedom

Deciphering the clues of financial freedom is akin to embarking on a quest for a hidden treasure, where the map is dotted with cryptic symbols, each representing a pivotal insight into the realm of wealth. This journey is not for the faint-hearted, as it demands a blend of courage, wisdom, and perseverance to navigate through the mazes of financial planning, investment strategies, and personal growth. Yet, the rewards of this quest are boundless, offering not just material wealth but the invaluable treasure of financial autonomy and peace of mind.

The first clue in this treasure hunt is the understanding of financial freedom itself. Financial freedom is often misconceived as the mere accumulation of wealth, but its essence lies in achieving an income that liberates one from the need to work for money. It's about creating a life where your time is your own, and your financial decisions are not driven by economic constraints but by personal choice and fulfillment. This profound understanding shifts the pursuit from amassing wealth to generating sustainable, passive income streams that support one's desired lifestyle.

Budgeting is the compass that guides this journey, a tool often underestimated in its power to unlock financial freedom. Mastering the art of budgeting is not merely about tracking expenses or cutting costs; it's about strategic allocation of resources to maximize happiness and fulfillment. It involves a delicate balance between living a life you enjoy today while saving and investing for the future you envision. Effective budgeting provides clarity, control, and a sense of empowerment, essential traits for anyone seeking financial independence.

Investing, the third clue, is the vessel that propels one towards financial freedom. The realm of investing is vast and varied, offering a plethora of options from stocks and bonds to real estate and beyond. The key is not just in choosing the right investments but in understanding the principles of compound interest, risk management, and diversification. Wise investing is about making your money work for you, creating a self-sustaining cycle of growth that builds wealth over time.

Debt management, a crucial but often daunting clue, holds the potential to make or break one's quest for financial freedom. The savvy adventurer knows that not all debt is created equal, distinguishing between debilitating high-interest debt and strategic debt that can lead to wealth accumulation, such as mortgages or business loans. Effective debt management involves prioritizing high-interest debts, understanding the terms and conditions of borrowing, and using credit wisely to leverage growth opportunities without falling into the trap of overleveraging.

The fifth clue lies in continuous learning and personal development. The landscape of personal finance is ever-evolving, with new opportunities, technologies, and strategies emerging constantly. The pursuit of financial freedom requires a commitment to lifelong learning, staying informed about economic trends, investment opportunities, and financial tools. This knowledge not only aids in making informed decisions but also in adapting to changes and challenges that may arise on the journey.

Income diversification is another vital clue, a strategy that spreads financial risk and opens multiple channels of income. The old adage of not putting all eggs in one basket holds particularly true in the context of financial freedom. Diversifying income sources, whether through side hustles, passive income ventures, or investments, ensures a more stable and resilient financial foundation, reducing dependence on a single income stream and providing a safety net in times of economic downturns.

Finally, the quest for financial freedom is deeply personal, and self-reflection is the compass that ensures one stays true to their path. It involves understanding personal values, goals, and what financial freedom means on an individual level. This introspection helps in aligning financial strategies with personal aspirations, ensuring that the pursuit of financial freedom is not just about achieving economic goals but about creating a fulfilling and meaningful life.

Deciphering the clues of financial freedom is an ongoing journey, one that requires patience, discipline, and a proactive approach to personal finance. It's a path that leads not just to financial wealth but to a life of autonomy, purpose, and peace, where financial decisions are driven by personal values and aspirations. Each clue uncovered on this quest brings one step closer to the ultimate treasure of financial freedom, a journey well worth the endeavor.

The Power of Defining your Treasure

In the quest for financial prosperity and personal fulfillment, defining your treasure is a pivotal step that often goes overlooked. This concept transcends the mere accumulation of wealth; it delves into the essence of what truly matters to an individual. It's about setting a vision for your life that aligns with your deepest values, aspirations, and what you define as success. The power of defining your treasure lies in its ability to transform a vague pursuit of wealth into a purpose-driven journey, making the path to financial freedom both meaningful and tailored to your unique life goals.

The first step in harnessing this power is self-reflection. This introspective process involves peeling back the layers of societal expectations, family pressures, and personal insecurities to uncover what truly brings you joy, fulfillment, and a sense of achievement. For some, this treasure might be financial independence to travel the world, for others, it could be the ability to support their family or contribute to causes close to their heart. The beauty of defining your treasure lies in its personalization; it's a treasure that holds value beyond monetary worth, encapsulating your passions, dreams, and the legacy you wish to leave behind.

Once the treasure is defined, it becomes a beacon, guiding financial decisions, career choices, and personal growth efforts. It acts as a motivational force, especially in times of uncertainty or when faced with financial challenges. The clarity of knowing what you're working towards can transform daunting obstacles into surmountable hurdles, imbuing each step of the journey with purpose and direction. This clarity not only fuels persistence but also fosters resilience, enabling individuals to navigate the volatile seas of life with a steadfast focus on their defined treasure.

The process of defining your treasure also encourages a holistic approach to goal setting. Instead of setting goals in isolation, they become interconnected steps towards a grand vision. This interconnectedness ensures that each financial decision, whether it's budgeting, investing, or saving, is made with an understanding of how it contributes to the larger picture. It prevents the common pitfall of short-sighted financial decisions that may offer immediate gratification but derail long-term objectives.

Moreover, defining your treasure cultivates a mindset of abundance rather than scarcity. When you have a clear vision of what you're striving for, you're more likely to recognize opportunities that align with your goals. This mindset shift is crucial in transforming how you view wealth creation; it becomes a journey of abundance where opportunities for growth and prosperity are abundant, rather than a zero-sum game where one's gain is another's loss.

In addition, the act of defining your treasure can lead to a more balanced and fulfilling life. When your financial goals are in harmony with your personal values and aspirations, you're less likely to fall into the trap of relentless pursuit of wealth at the expense of health, relationships, and personal well-being. This balance is essential for sustained success and happiness, as it ensures that the pursuit of financial freedom enriches your life rather than consuming it.

Furthermore, defining your treasure fosters a sense of accountability and ownership over your financial journey. It shifts the narrative from being a passive participant in the economic system to an active architect of your financial destiny. This sense of ownership is empowering, as it places the reins of your financial future firmly in your hands, guided by a clear vision of what you deem most valuable.

In essence, the power of defining your treasure lies in its ability to infuse your financial journey with purpose, clarity, and motivation. It transforms the pursuit of wealth from a generic goal into a personalized quest, rich with meaning and aligned with your deepest values and aspirations. By defining your treasure, you're not just setting financial goals; you're crafting a vision for your life that guides every decision, big or small, towards a future that resonates with your true self. It's a powerful tool that not only paves the way for financial success but also for a life filled with purpose, fulfillment, and joy.

Chapter 2: The Compass of goals

Setting Your Sails: Vision and Purpose

In the vast ocean of life, setting your sails towards the horizon of success requires more than mere ambition; it demands a clear vision and a defined purpose. These twin beacons serve as the guiding stars for individuals navigating the unpredictable waters of personal and professional growth. Vision provides the destination, a vivid picture of what one aspires to achieve, while purpose offers the why, the underlying reason that fuels the journey. Together, they create a powerful synergy that propels individuals forward, enabling them to harness their full potential and achieve their dreams.

Vision is the art of seeing the invisible, of imagining a future that is yet to be created. It's about painting a detailed picture in your mind's eye, one so vivid and compelling that it pulls you towards it. This vision could be personal, such as achieving financial independence, or professional, like becoming a leader in your field. What makes a vision powerful is not just the grandeur of the goal, but its clarity. The more detailed and specific your vision, the more real it becomes, and the stronger your desire to achieve it. This clarity acts as a mental compass, guiding your decisions, actions, and priorities, ensuring that every step you take moves you closer to your envisioned future.

Purpose, on the other hand, is the soul behind the vision. It's the deep-seated reason that gives your goals meaning and significance. Purpose answers the fundamental question of why you want to achieve your vision. It could stem from personal values, passions, or the desire to make a positive impact on the world. Purpose is what gives your journey depth and fulfillment, transforming the pursuit of goals from a self-centered endeavor to a mission that is bigger than oneself. It is the fuel that keeps the fire of motivation burning, even in the face of adversity and setbacks.

The interplay between vision and purpose is what sets truly successful individuals apart. Vision without purpose may lead to achievements, but they often feel hollow or unfulfilling. Purpose without a clear vision can result in passion that is directionless, like a ship adrift at sea. When combined, vision and purpose create a powerful synergy that not only directs your path but also infuses it with meaning, making the journey as rewarding as the destination.

Setting your sails with vision and purpose involves introspection and planning. It starts with allowing yourself to dream big, to envision a future without limits. This vision then needs to be articulated clearly, broken down into tangible goals and milestones. The next step is to connect this vision to your purpose, to delve deep into your core values and passions, and understand how your goals align with these principles. This alignment is crucial as it ensures that your path is not just leading you to success as defined by the world, but to a success that is deeply fulfilling and personally meaningful.

Moreover, setting your sails towards a vision and purpose-driven life demands resilience and adaptability. The journey is seldom a straight line; it is fraught with storms, high winds, and changing currents. Resilience allows you to weather the storms and stay the course, while adaptability enables you to adjust your sails as needed, ensuring that you remain aligned with your vision and purpose, even as circumstances change.

The power of setting your sails with vision and purpose cannot be overstated. It transforms the journey of life from a mere drift along the currents of circumstance to a purposeful voyage towards a chosen horizon. It empowers individuals to take control of their destiny, to live with intention and direction, and to achieve not just success, but fulfillment and joy. In the end, the strength of your vision and the depth of your purpose determine not just the distance you travel, but the richness of the journey itself.

Navigating through financial storms

Navigating through financial storms is an inevitable part of the journey towards economic stability and wealth creation. These storms, whether in the form of market downturns, unexpected job loss, or sudden personal emergencies, test the resilience and preparedness of even the most seasoned financial sailors. The key to weathering these storms lies not only in the strength of one's financial foundation but also in the agility and wisdom with which one responds to the tumultuous waves of uncertainty.

The first step in navigating financial storms is to recognize their inevitability. Much like the natural storms that sweep across the seas, financial turbulence is a part of the economic cycle. Accepting this reality prepares individuals to face financial challenges with a proactive mindset rather than a reactive one. It encourages the development of a financial buffer, an emergency fund that acts as a life raft, providing liquidity and peace of mind during times of economic distress. This fund should ideally cover several months of living expenses, ensuring that immediate financial obligations can be met without resorting to high-interest debt.

Diversification is the compass that guides individuals through financial storms. Just as a wise captain would not rely on a single sail to weather a storm, savvy individuals diversify their financial portfolio across various asset classes, industries, and geographies. This strategy mitigates risk by ensuring that a downturn in one sector does not capsize the entire financial ship. Diversification extends beyond investments; it also applies to income sources. Cultivating multiple streams of income can provide financial redundancy, much like having multiple engines in a ship, ensuring that if one fails, others can keep the financial vessel moving forward.

Financial literacy is the map that helps navigate through the murky waters of economic uncertainty. Understanding the basics of personal finance, investment principles, and economic indicators enables individuals to make informed decisions during turbulent times. It involves staying informed about market trends, recognizing the signs of a looming financial storm, and understanding the potential impact on one's personal finances. This knowledge empowers individuals to adjust their sails accordingly, whether it means rebalancing their investment portfolio, cutting back on non-essential expenses, or identifying new opportunities that arise in times of economic upheaval.

Flexibility and adaptability are the rudders that steer the financial ship through storms. Rigid financial plans that do not account for changing circumstances can lead to disastrous outcomes. The ability to adapt to changing financial landscapes, to pivot in response to new information, and to adjust financial goals and strategies is crucial. This might involve temporarily reducing investment contributions to bolster an emergency fund, renegotiating terms with creditors, or even changing investment strategies to capitalize on market conditions.

Emotional resilience is the anchor that holds firm in the face of financial storms. Economic downturns can be emotionally taxing, often evoking fear, anxiety, and panic. These emotions, if left unchecked, can lead to impulsive financial decisions that exacerbate the situation. Cultivating emotional resilience involves maintaining a long-term perspective, focusing on factors within one's control, and avoiding the temptation to make hasty decisions based on short-term market movements.

Community and support networks act as the crew that helps navigate through tough financial times. Sharing experiences, seeking advice, and leaning on the support of others can provide practical solutions and emotional comfort. Whether it's a professional financial advisor, a supportive family member, or a community of like-minded individuals, having a strong support network provides additional perspectives and resources that can be invaluable in navigating financial uncertainties.

In essence, navigating through financial storms requires a combination of preparation, knowledge, flexibility, and emotional resilience. It's about having the foresight to build a sturdy financial ship, the wisdom to chart a course through turbulent waters, and the courage to adjust the sails as the winds of fortune change. By embracing these principles, individuals can not only survive financial storms but emerge stronger, wiser, and more financially secure.

Landmarks of Success: Milestones to Treasure

In the journey of life and career, landmarks of success stand as milestones to treasure, signifying our progress, achievements, and the culmination of hard work and perseverance. These landmarks are not just markers of where we've been; they are beacons of inspiration, guiding us toward future aspirations and dreams. Recognizing and celebrating these milestones is crucial, for they are the tangible manifestations of our efforts, the embodiment of our challenges overcome, and the heralds of our potential to achieve even greater heights.

The first landmark in many success journeys is the moment of self-discovery, the point at which we gain a clear understanding of our passions, strengths, and purpose. This foundational milestone is critical, for it sets the direction of our journey, anchoring our goals and aspirations in the bedrock of our true selves. It's akin to finding the compass that will guide us through the tumultuous seas of life and career challenges, ensuring that our endeavors are aligned with our innermost values and aspirations.

Another significant landmark is the achievement of educational and professional qualifications. These milestones, marked by graduations, certifications, and promotions, are not merely ceremonial; they represent the accumulation of knowledge, skill, and expertise. They signify the transition from learning to application, from potential to action. Celebrating these achievements reminds us of the journey of growth and development we've undertaken, reinforcing the value of lifelong learning and the pursuit of excellence.

Overcoming obstacles and turning points constitute some of the most profound landmarks of success. These are the moments when, against all odds, we persevere through challenges, pivot from failure to opportunity, and emerge stronger and more resilient. These milestones are particularly treasurable, for they teach us invaluable lessons about grit, adaptability, and the indomitable human spirit.

They remind us that the path to success is not linear but a tapestry of setbacks and comebacks, each thread woven with the courage to continue.

The realization of personal and professional goals stands as another significant landmark. Whether it's launching a successful business, achieving a dream job, or completing a marathon, these achievements are the fruits of our labor, the dreams turned into reality through determination and hard work. They are reminders of our capability to set ambitious goals and see them through to fruition, serving as catalysts for setting new, even more, ambitious targets.

In the realm of success, the impact we have on others and the contributions we make to our communities and fields are landmarks as monumental as personal achievements. These milestones, characterized by mentorship, innovation, or philanthropy, transcend individual success, extending our legacy beyond personal gain. They reflect the essence of true success—the ability to uplift others, contribute to the greater good, and leave a lasting, positive mark on the world.

Finally, the balance and harmony we achieve between our personal and professional lives is a landmark of success that is often overlooked but is immensely valuable. This milestone is about finding fulfillment not just in our careers but in our relationships, hobbies, and personal well-being. It's a testament to our ability to nurture a holistic life where success is measured not only by professional achievements but by happiness, health, and meaningful connections.

Treating these landmarks of success as milestones to treasure involves more than mere acknowledgment; it requires reflection, gratitude, and celebration. It's about pausing to appreciate how far we've come, the lessons learned, and the growth experienced. Each landmark, whether a moment of triumph or a turning point, is a chapter in our unique story of success, a story that inspires not only ourselves but also those around us.

In essence, the landmarks of success are not just points on a timeline; they are the highlights of our life's narrative, each with its own story of ambition, challenge, and triumph. They are the moments that, when woven together, create a tapestry of a life well-lived, a career well-crafted, and a legacy well-established. Celebrating these milestones not only honors our past efforts but also ignites our passion for the adventures that lie ahead, in the continuous pursuit of excellence and fulfillment.

Chapter 3: the Crew of Allies

"Assembling Your Team of Mentors and Guides"

In the odyssey of personal and professional growth, assembling a team of mentors and guides stands as a pivotal chapter, a strategic move that can significantly alter the trajectory of one's journey. This assembly is not just about gathering a group of advisors; it's about curating a council of wisdom, experience, and insight that can illuminate the path ahead, challenge your perspectives, and propel you toward your goals. The act of selecting mentors and guides is both an art and a science, requiring careful consideration of the roles these individuals will play in your narrative of success.

The cornerstone of building this team is diversity—not just in terms of demographics but in expertise, experience, and outlook. A mentor who has navigated the complexities of your chosen field can offer invaluable industry-specific guidance, sharing the nuances of the trade and the secrets to navigating its labyrinthine pathways. They provide a roadmap of sorts, highlighting pitfalls to avoid and shortcuts worth taking. Yet, the journey to success is rarely a straight path, and it's here that mentors from varied backgrounds and disciplines bring their unique value. They introduce new paradigms, challenge industry dogmas, and encourage cross-pollination of ideas, fostering innovation and creativity.

Equally important is the inclusion of guides who offer not just professional insights but personal growth and development wisdom. These individuals may not be titans of industry but are giants in their understanding of human behavior, motivation, and resilience. They help in sculpting the softer skills—emotional intelligence, leadership, communication—that are critical in navigating the social complexities of the professional world. Their guidance is often the beacon that helps steer through the fog of career uncertainties and personal doubts.

The process of selecting these mentors and guides should be approached with intentionality, akin to casting characters for a pivotal role in a film. It requires identifying the gaps in your knowledge and experience, understanding your long-term goals, and recognizing the qualities you value in a mentor or guide. This selection is deeply personal; what works for one individual may not for another. Some may seek mentors who challenge and push them to their limits, while others may prefer a more nurturing and supportive approach.

Once assembled, the dynamics of this team should be nurtured with care and respect. The relationships with mentors and guides are built on mutual respect, trust, and a shared commitment to growth. It's a two-way street, where mentees must also bring value, whether through fresh perspectives, energy, or the willingness to dive into challenges. Active engagement, regular communication, and expressing gratitude for their time and insights are the bedrock of these relationships.

The digital age has expanded the horizons of mentorship, transcending geographical limitations and enabling connections with mentors and guides from around the globe. Virtual platforms, social media, and online communities offer unprecedented access to thought leaders, industry experts, and seasoned professionals. This digital landscape allows for a more dynamic and flexible mentorship experience, where guidance can be sought from multiple sources, each contributing a piece to the puzzle of personal and professional development.

In essence, assembling a team of mentors and guides is akin to building a personal board of directors, each member bringing their unique expertise, perspective, and wisdom to the table. This team becomes a pivotal force in one's journey, offering guidance through the tumultuous seas of career challenges, personal growth, and professional development. It's a testament to the power of collective wisdom, the importance of diverse perspectives, and the value of shared experiences. In the grand scheme of success, the guidance of mentors and the wisdom of guides are treasures to be sought, cherished, and utilized, propelling individuals toward their aspirations with confidence, clarity, and purpose.

The Role of a Mastermind Group in Your Journey

The concept of a mastermind group, though popularized by Napoleon Hill in his seminal work "Think and Grow Rich," traces its roots back to the dawn of collaborative thought. At its core, a mastermind group is a collective of like-minded individuals who come together with the purpose of mutual growth, support, and achievement of personal and professional goals. This synergy of minds creates a fertile ground for innovation, accountability, and transformation, playing a crucial role in the journey toward success.

The power of a mastermind group lies in its ability to harness diverse perspectives, experiences, and skills. Each member brings their unique insights, drawn from their own trials and triumphs, creating a rich tapestry of knowledge. This diversity is instrumental in providing multifaceted solutions to challenges, offering alternative viewpoints, and uncovering opportunities that may otherwise remain obscured. The collaborative environment fosters a culture of open exchange, where ideas can be shared freely, critiqued constructively, and refined collectively.

Accountability stands as one of the most significant benefits of participating in a mastermind group. In the solitary pursuit of goals, it's easy to lose sight of objectives, succumb to procrastination, or become entangled in the minutiae of daily tasks. The mastermind group acts as a compass, keeping members aligned with their larger vision. Regular meetings and check-ins create a structured framework for accountability, where members set goals, track progress, and are held responsible by the group. This external accountability mechanism is a powerful motivator, driving members to take consistent action toward their aspirations.

The journey towards personal and professional development is often fraught with challenges and setbacks. A mastermind group provides a supportive environment where members can share their struggles without fear of judgment. This emotional and moral support is invaluable, particularly during times of doubt or failure. The group serves as a sounding board, offering encouragement, empathy, and, when necessary, a dose of tough love. It's this support system that can be the difference between perseverance and abandonment of one's goals.

Networking and collaboration are natural byproducts of mastermind groups. By bringing together individuals from various backgrounds and industries, the group opens up a multitude of networking opportunities. These connections can lead to partnerships, client referrals, or simply the exchange of valuable contacts. Furthermore, the trust and rapport built within the group often pave the way for collaboration on projects or business ventures, leveraging the collective strength and resources of the members.

Continuous learning and personal growth are at the heart of the mastermind philosophy. The group operates on the principle that we are never done growing, and there is always something new to learn. Through regular meetings, workshops, and guest speakers, members are exposed to new knowledge, skills, and strategies. This environment of continuous education keeps members at the cutting edge of their respective fields and fosters a mindset of perpetual improvement.

The role of a mastermind group in one's journey is multifaceted, offering a blend of accountability, support, networking, and continuous learning. It's a platform where challenges can be transformed into opportunities, where ideas are cultivated into actionable plans, and where individuals come together to elevate not only themselves but each other. The collective wisdom of the group, combined with the structured approach to goal setting and problem-solving, makes the mastermind group a powerful catalyst for personal and professional development. For those committed to the path of growth and achievement, the mastermind group is not just a tool but an essential companion, guiding and supporting them through the complexities of their journey.

Networking: The Art of Building Wealth Together

Networking, often perceived merely as a professional tactic for career advancement, unfolds its true potential when viewed through the lens of collective wealth building. This nuanced approach to networking transcends the conventional exchange of business cards, evolving into a strategic collaboration that fosters mutual growth, knowledge sharing, and the creation of value that benefits all involved. The art of building wealth together through networking is a sophisticated dance of relationship building, trust cultivation, and the synergistic fusion of diverse skills and resources.

At the heart of this networking philosophy is the principle of reciprocity. The adage "give and you shall receive" holds profound truth in the context of wealth-building networks. The focus shifts from what one can gain to what one can contribute. This mindset fosters an environment of generosity, where sharing expertise, offering support, and connecting others become the foundational pillars. Such a culture not only enhances the collective wealth of the network but also strengthens individual positions within it, creating a virtuous cycle of giving and receiving.

The richness of a network is not measured by its size but by the depth of its relationships. Building wealth together requires more than superficial connections; it necessitates the cultivation of deep, meaningful relationships based on trust, respect, and mutual benefit. These relationships are built over time, through consistent interaction, shared experiences, and demonstrated reliability. It's within these deep connections that the most valuable exchanges occur, from insider insights and exclusive opportunities to strategic partnerships and collaborative ventures.

Diversity is the lifeblood of a wealth-building network. A homogenous group, while comfortable, is limited in its perspective and reach. A network that spans different industries, professions, and backgrounds brings together a kaleidoscope of ideas, opportunities, and resources. This diversity ignites innovation, opens new markets, and uncovers hidden opportunities for wealth creation. It challenges conventional thinking, encouraging members to explore new avenues for growth and investment.

Strategic networking involves positioning oneself within or at the intersection of multiple networks. This strategic position allows for the bridging of disparate groups, facilitating the flow of information, opportunities, and resources between them. Being a connector not only amplifies one's value within each network but also enhances the overall wealth-creating potential of the networks involved. This role requires a keen understanding of the needs and strengths of different networks and the ability to identify and create synergies between them.

The digital era has expanded the horizons of networking, breaking down geographical barriers and opening up a global stage for wealth-building collaborations. Online platforms, social media, and virtual communities offer unprecedented access to thought leaders, investors, and entrepreneurs worldwide. This digital network is a fertile ground for global collaborations, allowing for the pooling of international resources, knowledge, and markets to create wealth on a scale previously unimaginable.

Education and continuous learning are crucial for wealth building in networking. Staying informed about industry trends, economic shifts, and emerging technologies ensures longevity and prosperity for both individuals and networks.

Networking, when approached as the art of building wealth together, transforms from a mere professional strategy to a powerful catalyst for collective prosperity. It's an intricate dance of giving and receiving, underpinned by trust, diversity, strategic positioning, and continuous learning. In this collaborative endeavor, the wealth created transcends monetary gains, encompassing knowledge, opportunities, and a network of relationships that support and elevate each member. Through this collective approach, networking becomes not just a means to an end but a fulfilling journey of mutual growth and shared success.

Chapter 4: The Treasure Chest of Skills

Investing in Your Most Valuable Asset: Yourself

Investing in oneself is an enduring axiom of personal development, yet its significance extends far beyond the realms of motivational speeches and self-help books. This investment is the cornerstone of a fulfilling life and a prosperous career, embodying a broad spectrum of actions from enhancing one's education to nurturing physical and mental well-being. Recognizing and nurturing one's inherent value not only propels individuals towards their goals but also enriches their lives and the communities they inhabit.

Education and skill development stand at the forefront of self-investment. In an era marked by rapid technological advancements and shifting economic landscapes, the pursuit of knowledge remains a constant beacon. This quest for learning transcends traditional academic boundaries, embracing a lifelong commitment to growth. Whether through formal education, professional training, or self-directed learning, expanding one's knowledge base and skill set is pivotal. It equips individuals with the tools necessary to navigate the complexities of their professions, adapt to change, and seize emerging opportunities.

Mental and emotional well-being is another crucial facet of investing in oneself. In the relentless pursuit of external achievements, the significance of internal health often recedes into the background. Yet, mental resilience and emotional intelligence are the bedrock upon which professional success and personal satisfaction are built. Practices such as mindfulness, meditation, and therapy are not mere indulgences but essential investments in one's psychological foundation. They enhance decision-making abilities, stress management, and interpersonal skills, translating into a more balanced, productive, and fulfilling life.

Physical health, often celebrated for its immediate benefits, is equally a long-term investment in oneself. Regular exercise, a balanced diet, and adequate rest are the pillars of physical well-being. This trinity of health not only bolsters daily energy levels and productivity but also wards off the long-term detriments of a sedentary lifestyle. The correlation between physical health and mental acuity is well-documented, with each reinforcing the other, creating a virtuous cycle of overall well-being.

Personal relationships and networks constitute another dimension of self-investment. Cultivating meaningful connections and surrounding oneself with a supportive and inspiring community amplifies personal growth. These relationships serve as mirrors, reflecting our values, aspirations, and areas for improvement. They provide a safety net in times of adversity, a sounding board for ideas, and a source of diverse perspectives. Investing time and energy in nurturing these connections ensures a rich tapestry of personal and professional support, invaluable in the journey of life.

Personal finance and wealth management, often relegated to the peripheries of self-care, are integral to self-investment. Financial literacy empowers individuals to make informed decisions, safeguarding their future and enabling the pursuit of their dreams. Understanding the basics of budgeting, saving, investing, and wealth protection is not just about accumulating wealth but about ensuring freedom and choices throughout one's life.

Creative pursuits and hobbies offer a respite from the rigors of professional endeavors, fostering a sense of joy and fulfillment. These activities, whether artistic, athletic, or intellectual, enrich the soul and spark creativity. They provide a counterbalance to work, reducing burnout and enhancing overall life satisfaction. Investing in these pursuits is a testament to the multifaceted nature of personal growth, acknowledging that fulfillment stems from a mosaic of experiences.

Investing in oneself is a multifaceted endeavor, encompassing the continuous development of mind, body, and spirit. It's about recognizing one's inherent worth and potential, then taking deliberate steps to nurture, challenge, and fulfill that potential. This investment lays the foundation for not just professional success but a rich, balanced, and rewarding life. It's a commitment to oneself that pays dividends in every aspect of existence, from career achievements to personal happiness and societal contributions.

Mastering the Skills of Wealth Generation

Mastering the skills of wealth generation is akin to navigating a complex labyrinth, where strategic thinking, informed decision-making, and continuous adaptation are key to finding the path to financial prosperity. This journey transcends the mere accumulation of assets; it involves cultivating a mindset, honing a set of skills, and applying principles that collectively contribute to the creation and sustenance of wealth. At the heart of this endeavor lies the understanding that wealth generation is not a product of happenstance but the result of deliberate actions and informed choices.

Financial literacy forms the cornerstone of wealth generation skills. It encompasses a deep understanding of financial concepts, market dynamics, and economic indicators, empowering individuals to make decisions that align with their long-term financial goals. This knowledge base includes, but is not limited to, budgeting, investing, saving, and debt management. Mastery over these areas allows individuals to navigate the financial landscape with confidence, making choices that compound over time to build a solid foundation of wealth.

Investing is another critical skill in the wealth generation arsenal. It involves not just the allocation of financial resources into various asset classes but also the strategic diversification to mitigate risk and maximize returns. Mastery in investing requires a thorough understanding of different investment vehicles, market trends, and risk assessment techniques. It also calls for a disciplined approach to investing, characterized by regular contributions, long-term horizons, and the resilience to withstand market volatilities without succumbing to impulsive decisions.

Entrepreneurship and the ability to identify and capitalize on opportunities are pivotal in wealth generation. This skill set extends beyond starting and running a business; it encompasses innovation, risk-taking, and the ability to turn ideas into profitable ventures. Entrepreneurs contribute to wealth generation not only for themselves but also for their employees, stakeholders, and the broader economy. The entrepreneurial journey involves continuous learning, adaptability, and the courage to venture into the unknown, armed with the conviction of one's vision and the resilience to persevere through challenges.

Effective communication and negotiation skills play a significant role in wealth generation. Whether it's negotiating a salary, discussing terms with suppliers, or networking with potential investors, the ability to communicate clearly, persuasively, and effectively can significantly impact financial outcomes. These skills facilitate the forging of valuable relationships, the establishment of trust, and the creation of mutually beneficial agreements, all of which are critical components of wealth generation.

Time management and productivity are integral to mastering wealth generation. The adage "time is money" holds profound truth in this context, where efficient use of time translates into greater opportunities for wealth creation. Mastering time management involves prioritizing tasks, setting and achieving goals, and eliminating inefficiencies, thereby maximizing the potential for income generation and wealth accumulation.

Emotional intelligence, though often overlooked, is a crucial skill in wealth generation. It involves the ability to manage one's emotions, empathize with others, and navigate social complexities. High emotional intelligence contributes to better decision-making, stronger relationships, and the resilience to face financial ups and downs without succumbing to stress or impulsive decisions.

Mastering the skills of wealth generation is a multifaceted process that involves a combination of financial acumen, strategic thinking, interpersonal skills, and personal discipline. It requires a commitment to continuous learning, an openness to adapt, and the resilience to persevere through the inevitable challenges that accompany the journey to financial prosperity. By cultivating these skills, individuals can unlock their potential for wealth generation, setting the stage for financial independence and the ability to achieve their most ambitious life goals.

The Magic of Continuous Learning and Adaptation

The magic of continuous learning and adaptation lies at the heart of personal and professional evolution, serving as the catalyst for growth, innovation, and resilience in an ever-changing world. This relentless pursuit of knowledge and flexibility in the face of new challenges not only enriches one's life with diverse experiences and skills but also ensures relevance and competitiveness in today's dynamic landscape. Embracing continuous learning and adaptation is akin to setting sail on a voyage of discovery, where each new skill acquired and each adjustment made charts a course toward uncharted territories of opportunity and self-fulfillment.

In the realm of continuous learning, the quest for knowledge is boundless, transcending traditional educational paradigms to encompass a lifelong commitment to exploration and curiosity. This journey is fueled by the understanding that the reservoir of human knowledge is vast and ever-expanding, with innovations, discoveries, and insights constantly reshaping the world around us. Engaging in continuous learning means actively seeking out new information, skills, and experiences, whether through formal education, self-directed study, professional development, or hands-on experiences. It's about remaining a perpetual student, open to the lessons that every situation, every interaction, and every challenge has to offer.

The transformative power of continuous learning lies not just in the accumulation of knowledge, but in the application and integration of this knowledge into one's life and work. It involves not only understanding theories and concepts but also applying them creatively to solve problems, innovate, and improve existing practices. This application of knowledge fosters a culture of innovation, where the status quo is continuously challenged and improved upon, driving progress and excellence in every endeavor.

Adaptation, the complementary force to continuous learning, is the ability to remain flexible and responsive to change. In a world characterized by rapid technological advancements, shifting market dynamics, and evolving societal norms, the capacity to adapt is invaluable. It requires an openness to change, a willingness to question and revise one's assumptions and strategies, and the agility to pivot when circumstances demand it. Adaptation is about embracing change not as a threat but as an opportunity for growth and development.

The synergy between continuous learning and adaptation is particularly evident in the face of adversity or failure. Instead of being roadblocks, these challenges become stepping stones, opportunities for learning and growth. The continuous learner analyzes setbacks, extracts lessons, and applies these insights to future endeavors, while the adept adapter views change and failure as catalysts for innovation and redirection. This proactive and positive approach to challenges fosters resilience, ensuring that individuals and organizations not only survive but thrive in the face of adversity.

Moreover, continuous learning and adaptation have a profound impact on personal fulfillment and job satisfaction. The pursuit of new knowledge and skills keeps the mind active and engaged, fostering a sense of achievement and confidence. Similarly, the ability to adapt to new roles, responsibilities, and environments keeps one's career dynamic and exciting, preventing stagnation and promoting a sense of progress and renewal.

In the professional realm, the magic of continuous learning and adaptation is a key differentiator in a crowded and competitive marketplace. It equips individuals with a broad and diverse skill set, fosters innovative thinking, and cultivates a proactive mindset that is invaluable in identifying and seizing new opportunities. Organizations that foster a culture of continuous learning and adaptability are better positioned to navigate the complexities of the modern business landscape, driving growth, innovation, and long-term success.

In essence, the magic of continuous learning and adaptation is not just about acquiring knowledge or responding to change; it's about embracing a philosophy of life that values growth, resilience, and the endless pursuit of excellence. It's a commitment to never stop growing, exploring, and evolving, ensuring that both individuals and organizations remain relevant, competitive, and fulfilled in an ever-changing world.

Chapter 5: Islands of Opportunity

Identifying Lucrative Ventures in Uncharted Waters

Venturing into uncharted waters to identify lucrative opportunities is a bold move that embodies the spirit of innovation and entrepreneurship. In a world where conventional paths are increasingly crowded and competitive, the allure of untapped markets and emerging industries offers a beacon of potential for those daring enough to explore them. This endeavor, while fraught with uncertainty and risk, can yield unparalleled rewards for those who navigate these waters with a keen eye for opportunity, a strategic mindset, and an unwavering resilience.

The first step in this voyage is the cultivation of a visionary perspective. This involves looking beyond the current market trends and demands to anticipate future needs and developments. Visionaries thrive on the periphery of current industry boundaries, where the seeds of future markets lie dormant, waiting for the right combination of insight and innovation to bring them to fruition. This forward-thinking approach requires not just an understanding of existing markets but also an imaginative leap into the possibilities of what could be, driven by technological advancements, societal shifts, and global trends.

Market research and analysis form the compass for navigating these uncharted waters. Comprehensive research provides a foundation for understanding the dynamics of potential markets, including customer needs, existing gaps, and competitive landscapes. This involves delving into industry reports, academic research, and market forecasts, as well as engaging with potential consumers and industry experts. Such in-depth exploration is crucial for validating the viability of ventures in new markets and for refining business models to meet the unique demands of these emerging opportunities.

Technological innovation is often the sail that propels ventures into new territories. Leveraging cutting-edge technologies can provide a significant advantage in developing novel solutions and accessing untapped markets. From blockchain and artificial intelligence to renewable energy and biotech, emerging technologies offer a plethora of opportunities for creating value in new and innovative ways. Entrepreneurs who master these technologies can unlock new applications and services, addressing unmet needs and creating markets where none existed before.

Risk assessment and management are the anchors of any venture into uncharted territories. While the potential for high returns is significant, so too is the risk of failure. A comprehensive risk management strategy, including thorough market testing, phased investments, and contingency planning, is essential for navigating these uncertainties. This pragmatic approach allows entrepreneurs to mitigate potential losses, learn from market feedback, and pivot strategies as necessary, ensuring that the journey into new markets is both calculated and adaptable.

Building a diverse and skilled team is the crew that steers the ship toward success. Ventures into new markets require a multidisciplinary approach, combining expertise from various fields to tackle the unique challenges and opportunities these markets present. A team that brings together industry experts, technology specialists, and creative thinkers can provide the comprehensive skill set and innovative mindset required to capitalize on emerging opportunities.

Networking and strategic partnerships can also provide valuable navigational aids in exploring new markets. Collaborations with established players, industry associations, or research institutions can offer critical insights, resources, and credibility to ventures in uncharted waters. These alliances can be instrumental in overcoming initial barriers to entry, accelerating market penetration, and scaling the business.

Identifying lucrative ventures in uncharted waters is a complex and challenging endeavor, requiring a blend of vision, research, innovation, risk management, teamwork, and strategic alliances.

Entrepreneurs who embark on this journey must be prepared to face the uncertainties and challenges inherent in exploring new territories. Yet, for those with the courage to venture beyond the familiar, the uncharted waters of emerging markets hold the promise of untold opportunities and the potential for groundbreaking success.

Top Examples of Lucrative Ventures

1. Renewable Energy Solutions

The global push towards sustainability has opened vast opportunities in the renewable energy sector. Ventures like solar panel installations, wind farms, and bioenergy production are not just environmentally beneficial; they're also increasingly profitable. Innovations in energy storage, such as advanced battery systems, further enhance the viability and attractiveness of renewable energy solutions. These ventures tap into a growing market demand for clean, sustainable, and affordable energy, driven by both environmental concerns and the economic benefits of reduced energy costs.

2. HealthTech Innovations

The healthcare industry is ripe for disruption, with technology playing a pivotal role. HealthTech ventures range from telemedicine platforms, which break down geographical barriers to healthcare access, to wearable health monitors that provide real-time data on vital signs. Other innovations include AI-driven diagnostics tools that offer faster, more accurate diagnoses and personalized medicine, where treatments are tailored to the individual's genetic makeup. These ventures address critical healthcare challenges, improve patient outcomes, and have the potential to significantly reduce healthcare costs.

3. FinTech Startups

Financial technology, or FinTech, has transformed the way we manage and interact with our finances. Ventures in this space include mobile payment solutions, peer-to-peer lending platforms, and personal finance apps that offer users greater control over their finances. Cryptocurrency exchanges and blockchain-based financial services are also part of this burgeoning sector. These startups are democratizing financial services, making them more accessible, efficient, and secure, and often at a lower cost than traditional financial institutions.

4. EdTech Platforms

Education technology has revolutionized learning, making education more accessible and personalized. Lucrative ventures include online learning platforms that offer courses from institutions around the world, language learning apps, and virtual tutoring services. There's also a significant push towards gamification in education, where game design elements are used to enhance learning experiences. These ventures cater to a growing demand for flexible, self-paced learning options that accommodate diverse learning styles and needs.

5. Sustainable Consumer Goods

The consumer goods sector is witnessing a surge in demand for sustainable, eco-friendly products. Ventures in this space range from sustainable fashion, where materials are ethically sourced and produced, to zero-waste products that eliminate the use of plastic. There's also a growing market for plant-based foods, which cater to both environmental and health-conscious consumers. These ventures tap into a growing consumer awareness and concern for the environment, offering products that align with their values.

6. Smart Home Technologies

The rise of the Internet of Things (IoT) has paved the way for smart home technologies, where household devices are interconnected and can be remotely controlled. Ventures in this area include smart thermostats, security systems, and lighting solutions that enhance home efficiency, security, and convenience. The market for smart home technologies is expanding rapidly, driven by advances in IoT, AI, and consumer demand for convenience and energy efficiency.

Each of these ventures represents a confluence of innovation, market demand, and the potential for significant impact. Entrepreneurs venturing into these areas must navigate challenges including market education, regulatory landscapes, and technological complexities. However, with the right approach, these ventures offer substantial opportunities for growth and profitability.

Risk and Reward: The Adventurer's Dilemma

The concept of risk and reward lies at the very heart of the adventurer's dilemma, a fundamental dynamic that governs not just the world of exploration and discovery, but also the realms of business, investment, and personal growth. This age-old quandary posits a simple yet profound question: How much risk is one willing to take for the potential of a corresponding reward? The delicate balance between these two forces shapes decisions, strategies, and ultimately, the outcomes of ventures both great and small.

At the core of the adventurer's dilemma is the understanding that risk and reward are inextricably linked, with the potential for higher returns often accompanied by increased levels of risk. This relationship is a fundamental principle in the world of finance, encapsulated by the risk-return tradeoff, which asserts that the possibility of higher profits comes with a greater chance of loss. However, this principle extends far beyond the financial markets, permeating every decision that involves uncertainty and the potential for variable outcomes.

The adventurer's spirit, whether in the context of exploring uncharted territories, launching a startup, or embarking on a personal journey of self-discovery, requires a nuanced understanding of this risk-reward dynamic. It involves evaluating the potential benefits of a venture against the possible drawbacks, assessing not just the tangible outcomes but also the intangible elements such as personal growth, fulfillment, and the expansion of one's horizons.

Risk assessment, therefore, becomes a critical skill for the modern adventurer. It involves a thorough analysis of the potential risks involved in a venture, from financial losses and resource depletion to reputational damage and personal well-being. This assessment is not a one-time task but a continuous process that adapts as circumstances change and new information comes to light. Effective risk management strategies, including diversification, hedging, and the setting of stop-loss points, are essential tools in the adventurer's arsenal, helping to mitigate potential losses while still pursuing the lure of substantial rewards.

Yet, the adventurer's dilemma is not solely a matter of logic and calculation. It also engages the emotional and psychological dimensions of risk-taking. The thrill of potential discovery and success must be balanced against the fear of failure, loss, and the unknown. Emotional resilience and the ability to maintain a steady course in the face of uncertainty are hallmark traits of those who navigate this dilemma successfully. The psychological aspect of risk involves not just the capacity to endure setbacks but also the wisdom to know when to push forward and when to retreat.

The concept of calculated risks introduces a strategic element to the adventurer's dilemma. Rather than shying away from all risks, the savvy adventurer learns to take calculated risks—those where the potential rewards justify the potential losses. This approach involves not just an assessment of the odds but also the preparation and planning to enhance the chances of success and minimize the potential for adverse outcomes.

Innovation and creativity are often born from the willingness to embrace risk. History is replete with examples of adventurers, entrepreneurs, and pioneers who took bold risks and reaped substantial rewards, not just for themselves but for society at large. These individuals understood that progress and breakthroughs are seldom achieved by playing it safe but rather by venturing into the unknown with courage and conviction.

The adventurer's dilemma, with its intricate dance between risk and reward, challenges individuals to confront their fears, assess their tolerance for uncertainty, and make decisions that balance the potential for gain against the possibility of loss. It is a fundamental aspect of the human experience, driving exploration, innovation, and the continual quest for growth. Navigating this delicate balance requires a blend of knowledge, intuition, and courage, as each adventurer charts their unique course through the uncertain waters of risk and reward.

The Art of Timing in Wealth Accumulation

The art of timing in wealth accumulation is a nuanced strategy that transcends mere financial management; it embodies the intricate dance of making strategic decisions that align with the rhythms of markets, life stages, and economic cycles. This sophisticated approach requires not only an understanding of financial principles but also an intuitive sense of when to act, when to hold steady, and when to pivot. It's about recognizing that timing can be as crucial as the investment itself, turning good opportunities into outstanding ones.

In the realm of investing, the timing of market entry and exit plays a pivotal role. The adage "buy low, sell high" captures the essence of market timing, yet its application is anything but simple. It involves a deep understanding of market trends, economic indicators, and the psychological factors that drive market movements. Successful investors often employ a combination of technical analysis, fundamental analysis, and economic insights to make informed decisions about when to enter or exit a market. However, it's not about attempting to time the market perfectly—a feat many consider impossible—but about making informed decisions that increase the likelihood of favorable outcomes.

The art of timing also extends to life stage financial planning. Each phase of life brings with it specific financial needs, goals, and opportunities. In the early career stage, the focus may be on debt reduction, savings, and the initiation of retirement accounts. As individuals progress in their careers and increase their earning potential, the emphasis shifts to wealth accumulation, investment diversification, and perhaps real estate acquisition. Approaching retirement, the strategy pivots again towards wealth preservation, income generation, and estate planning. Understanding and anticipating these life stage transitions allows for the strategic allocation of resources, ensuring that financial strategies are aligned with changing needs and goals.

Economic cycles also play a crucial role in the timing of wealth accumulation efforts. Economic expansions, recessions, and recoveries each present unique challenges and opportunities for investors. For instance, recessions, while often viewed negatively, can present opportunities to acquire valuable assets at lower prices. Conversely, periods of economic expansion might offer favorable conditions for selling assets or launching new ventures. Astute investors monitor these economic cycles, adapting their strategies to capitalize on the opportunities each phase presents.

The timing of wealth accumulation is also influenced by personal circumstances and goals. Major life events such as marriage, the birth of a child, or a career change can significantly impact one's financial planning and investment strategies. Similarly, personal goals, whether short-term like purchasing a home or long-term like securing a comfortable retirement, require timely planning and execution. Balancing these personal factors with broader economic and market conditions is a delicate endeavor, necessitating flexibility and foresight in financial planning.

Moreover, the psychological aspect of timing cannot be overlooked. The emotional fortitude to withstand market volatility, resist the herd mentality, and maintain a long-term perspective is essential. The fear of missing out (FOMO) or panic selling during downturns can derail even the most well-thought-out investment strategies. Cultivating a disciplined approach, grounded in a solid understanding of one's financial goals and risk tolerance, is key to navigating these emotional challenges.

In essence, the art of timing in wealth accumulation is a multifaceted discipline that integrates financial acumen, strategic planning, and psychological resilience. It's not about precise predictions or rigid adherence to timelines but about the judicious application of knowledge, intuition, and patience. By mastering this art, individuals can enhance their potential for wealth accumulation, turning the passage of time into a powerful ally in the quest for financial prosperity.

Chapter 6: The Pirates of Debt

Navigating Through the Perils of Bad Debt

Navigating through the perils of bad debt is akin to steering a ship through treacherous waters, where the hazards of high interest rates and the undertow of compounding payments threaten to capsize financial stability. Bad debt, characterized by its detrimental impact on financial health and its often high-cost nature, can quickly spiral out of control if not managed wisely. Understanding the intricacies of bad debt and employing strategic measures to mitigate its impact is crucial for maintaining financial equilibrium and charting a course toward fiscal solvency.

The first step in this journey is the recognition and differentiation of bad debt from potentially 'good' debt. While the latter can be an investment that leads to long-term value, such as a mortgage for a home that appreciates or a loan for education that increases earning potential, bad debt typically offers no return and often finances depreciating assets or consumables. High-interest credit card debt, payday loans, and high-rate personal loans often fall into this perilous category, offering fleeting gratification at the cost of long-term financial strain.

Once identified, the consolidation of bad debts can serve as an effective strategy to mitigate their impact. This approach involves combining multiple high-interest debts into a single, lower-interest loan, simplifying payments, and reducing the amount paid in interest over time. Debt consolidation loans or balance transfer credit cards with low introductory rates can provide much-needed reprieve, but they require discipline to ensure that this strategy doesn't become a means to accumulate more debt.

Negotiation with creditors presents another avenue for navigating the perils of bad debt. Many borrowers are unaware that lenders may be willing to negotiate terms to avoid the potential loss of default. This could involve lowering interest rates, waiving fees, or restructuring the repayment plan to more manageable terms. Open communication with creditors, expressing a genuine intention to repay the debt, can open doors to more favorable repayment conditions.

Budgeting plays a pivotal role in managing bad debt. Creating and adhering to a realistic budget that prioritizes debt repayment can free up additional funds to tackle high-interest debts more aggressively. This often involves cutting non-essential expenses and reallocating those funds towards debt repayment, a practice known as the 'snowball' or 'avalanche' method, depending on whether the focus is on clearing smallest debts first for psychological wins or targeting high-interest debts to reduce overall interest paid.

An often-overlooked aspect of navigating bad debt is the importance of building an emergency fund, even while in debt. While it may seem counterintuitive to save when facing high-interest debt, having a financial cushion can prevent the need to incur additional debt in the face of unforeseen expenses, breaking the cycle of debt accumulation.

Education and financial literacy are the compasses by which individuals can steer clear of future bad debts. Understanding the cost of credit, the impact of compound interest, and the importance of reading and understanding loan agreements can empower individuals to make informed financial decisions, avoiding the pitfalls of bad debt.

Lastly, seeking professional advice from financial advisors or credit counseling services can provide tailored strategies and support for those overwhelmed by bad debt. These professionals can offer insights into debt management plans, bankruptcy as a last resort, and strategies to rebuild credit health post-debt.

Navigating through the perils of bad debt requires a multifaceted approach, combining strategic financial planning, disciplined budgeting, and proactive communication with creditors. By employing these strategies, individuals can chart a course toward financial stability, gradually steering away from the treacherous waters of bad debt toward the calmer seas of financial freedom.

Strategies to Combat Financial Leeches

In the realm of personal finance, "financial leeches" refer to those recurring, often unnoticed expenses or habits that slowly drain your resources, undermining your financial health and wealth accumulation efforts. These can range from high-interest debts and unnecessary subscriptions to energy-inefficient appliances and costly personal habits. Identifying and combating these financial leeches is crucial for maintaining a healthy financial ecosystem and ensuring that your resources are allocated towards achieving your financial goals.

The first step in combating financial leeches is thorough financial auditing. This involves meticulously reviewing bank statements, bills, and expenses to identify where your money is going each month. It's often surprising to discover how much is being siphoned off by seemingly inconsequential expenses, be it daily gourmet coffees or impulse online purchases. This audit provides a clear picture of your financial outflows and highlights areas where leeches may be lurking.

Once identified, tackling high-interest debt should be a priority. Debts, particularly those with high interest rates like credit card balances, can rapidly escalate due to compounding interest, becoming significant financial burdens. Strategies such as debt consolidation, balance transfers to lower interest rate cards, or employing the debt snowball or avalanche methods can be effective in managing and eventually eliminating these debts. The key is to prevent these debts from continuously draining your financial reserves.

Subscriptions and memberships represent another common financial leech. In today's digital age, it's easy to accumulate a variety of subscriptions, from streaming services to fitness apps. However, not all of these subscriptions are utilized sufficiently to justify their cost. Evaluating the value and usage of each subscription and canceling those that do not provide sufficient value can stem the flow of funds towards these silent financial drains.

Lifestyle inflation, the tendency to increase spending as income rises, can also act as a financial leech, preventing significant wealth accumulation despite increases in earning. Maintaining a disciplined approach to spending, regardless of income hikes, and prioritizing savings and investment can counteract lifestyle inflation. This doesn't mean living frugally at all times but making conscious decisions about spending that align with long-term financial objectives.

Energy inefficiency in homes is a less obvious but equally potent financial leech. Outdated appliances, poor insulation, and energy-inefficient lighting can lead to unnecessarily high utility bills. Investing in energy-efficient appliances, LED lighting, and home insulation can reduce these costs over time, freeing up more funds for savings and investments.

Personal habits, such as dining out frequently, expensive hobbies, or luxury shopping, can also act as financial leeches if not kept in check. Setting a budget for discretionary spending and finding cost-effective alternatives for expensive habits can help manage these costs without sacrificing enjoyment and lifestyle quality.

Finally, proactive financial planning is essential in combating financial leeches. This involves setting clear financial goals, creating a budget that aligns with these goals, and regularly reviewing and adjusting the budget as needed. Employing tools such as automatic savings plans and investment contributions can also ensure that money is directed towards wealth-building activities before it can be eroded by financial leeches.

In summary, combating financial leeches requires a combination of vigilance, strategic action, and disciplined financial management. By identifying and addressing these drains on your resources, you can safeguard your financial health, ensuring that your money is working towards building a secure and prosperous financial future.

Scan the QR code for a little bounty.

Building Your Defense: The Emergency Fund

In the unpredictable theater of life, financial uncertainties are akin to uninvited specters that loom over one's peace of mind. The emergency fund, a financial bulwark, stands as a testament to prudent foresight, offering a buffer against the unforeseen tempests of life. This strategic reserve is more than a mere accumulation of funds; it is a deliberate construction of financial resilience, enabling individuals to navigate through turbulent times without compromising their long-term financial health.

The inception of an emergency fund begins with the acknowledgment of life's inherent unpredictability. From sudden medical emergencies and unexpected job losses to urgent home repairs and unforeseen travel needs, life's contingencies are varied and inevitable. An emergency fund acts as a financial shock absorber, providing immediate liquidity to address these crises without resorting to high-interest debt options such as credit cards or personal loans, which can exacerbate financial strain.

Determining the size of the emergency fund is a pivotal step in building this financial defense. Conventional wisdom suggests an ideal reserve covering three to six months' worth of living expenses, offering a substantial buffer to weather most financial storms. However, the exact amount can vary based on individual circumstances, including job stability, the presence of dependents, and existing financial obligations. For those with more volatile income streams or higher financial commitments, a more substantial fund may be warranted to ensure adequate coverage.

The creation of an emergency fund is a disciplined endeavor, necessitating a systematic approach to savings. This often involves setting clear, achievable goals and employing a consistent savings strategy. Automating transfers to a dedicated emergency savings account can simplify this process, ensuring regular contributions without the need for manual intervention. This account should be separate from regular checking or savings accounts to avoid the temptation of dipping into these funds for non-emergency purposes.

Liquidity is a cornerstone characteristic of an effective emergency fund. The primary purpose of these reserves is to provide immediate access to funds in times of need, making the choice of savings vehicle critically important. High-yield savings accounts, money market accounts, or short-term certificates of deposit can offer a balance between accessibility and earning modest interest, ensuring that the emergency fund remains readily available while still growing over time.

Maintaining the sanctity of the emergency fund is crucial for its effectiveness. These funds should be earmarked exclusively for true emergencies, distinct from foreseeable expenses or discretionary spending. Establishing clear criteria for what constitutes an emergency can help safeguard against the gradual erosion of this financial safety net for non-urgent expenditures.

In addition to providing financial security, an emergency fund also offers profound psychological benefits. The knowledge that one has a financial cushion to fall back on in times of crisis can alleviate stress and anxiety, fostering a sense of security and well-being. This peace of mind is invaluable, enabling individuals to make rational, measured decisions even in the face of unexpected challenges.

Furthermore, the process of building and maintaining an emergency fund can instill valuable financial habits. The discipline, foresight, and financial management skills developed through this process can have far-reaching benefits, enhancing overall financial literacy and paving the way for more informed and deliberate financial decisions in the future.

In summary, building an emergency fund is a fundamental component of a robust financial plan, offering a defensive bastion against life's unforeseen challenges. It requires careful planning, consistent effort, and disciplined management, but the security and peace of mind it provides are immeasurable. In the grand strategy of financial well-being, an emergency fund is not merely an option but an imperative, ensuring that individuals are well-equipped to face life's vicissitudes with confidence and resilience.

Chapter 7: The Mermaids of Spending

The Siren Call of Impulse Buying

The siren call of impulse buying, with its alluring melody, tempts even the most disciplined among us, leading us into the treacherous waters of financial instability and regret. This phenomenon, characterized by the spontaneous, unplanned decision to purchase, often strikes under the hypnotic glow of store lights or the seductive ease of a "one-click" online transaction. Like the mythical sirens whose enchanting music lured sailors to their doom, impulse buying beckons with the promise of immediate gratification, only to leave a trail of disrupted budgets and cluttered spaces in its wake.

The mechanisms behind impulse buying are complex, intertwining psychological triggers with strategic marketing tactics. Retail environments, both physical and digital, are meticulously designed to capitalize on emotional responses, leveraging colors, layouts, and promotions to evoke feelings of desire, urgency, and exclusivity. Online platforms amplify this effect with algorithms that tailor advertisements and recommendations to individual preferences, creating a personalized web of temptation that is difficult to escape.

Emotional states play a pivotal role in susceptibility to impulse purchases. Moments of euphoria can lead to celebratory spending, a way to prolong the bliss of positive news or personal achievements. Conversely, periods of stress, anxiety, or sadness may trigger comfort buying, where the act of purchasing serves as a temporary salve for emotional discomfort. This emotional spending, though momentarily soothing, often leads to buyer's remorse once the initial rush fades and the reality of the expenditure sets in.

Social influences further exacerbate the impulse to buy. The pervasive nature of social media, with its curated showcases of lifestyle and consumption, fuels a sense of keeping up with the proverbial Joneses. The fear of missing out (FOMO) on trends, gadgets, or experiences can propel individuals into making hasty purchases, driven by the desire to belong and be perceived in a certain light by peers and society.

Combatting the siren call of impulse buying requires a multifaceted strategy, rooted in awareness, planning, and discipline. Recognizing personal triggers, whether emotional states, environments, or social pressures, is the first step in developing a defense against impulsive spending. This awareness enables individuals to identify moments of vulnerability and employ tactics to resist the urge to purchase.

Setting clear financial goals and budgets provides a framework that can curb impulse buying. When every dollar is accounted for and aligned with long-term objectives, the cost of impulsive purchases becomes more evident, not just in monetary terms but in the delay or derailment of achieving financial milestones. Employing a waiting period rule, where decisions on non-essential purchases are deferred for a set time, can also dampen the immediacy of impulse buying, allowing time for rational evaluation over emotional reaction.

Mindful consumption practices, emphasizing the value of experiences over possessions and the quality of goods over quantity, can shift perspectives on spending. This approach fosters a deeper appreciation for what one already owns and reduces the allure of new, unnecessary acquisitions.

Moreover, the cultivation of financial literacy is a potent tool in resisting impulse buying. Understanding the true cost of debt, the impact of small purchases on long-term savings, and the principles of wealth accumulation can transform one's approach to spending, prioritizing financial health over fleeting pleasures.

In navigating the enticing yet perilous waters of impulse buying, individuals must arm themselves with strategies that foster mindfulness, discipline, and a deep-seated commitment to their financial well-being. By heeding the lessons of those who have succumbed to and overcome the lure of impulsive spending, one can chart a course toward a more stable and fulfilling financial future, free from the chains of momentary whims.

Budgeting: Your Map to Controlled Expenditures

Budgeting is a crucial financial management tool that simplifies income, expenses, and savings, enabling conscious decision-making and aligning daily spending with long-term financial goals, providing clarity and control.

The foundational step in budgeting involves a thorough assessment of income. This includes not just the primary source, such as a salary, but also any ancillary streams like side hustles, investments, or rental income. A clear understanding of total monthly income sets the stage for informed allocation towards various spending and saving categories, ensuring that expenditures never outpace earnings.

Following income, a deep dive into expenses is essential. Expenses are broadly categorized into fixed and variable. Fixed expenses, such as rent or mortgage, insurance premiums, and loan payments, are typically non-negotiable and recur monthly with little fluctuation. Variable expenses, however, such as groceries, entertainment, and discretionary purchases, can fluctuate widely and offer greater room for adjustment. Distinguishing between these helps in identifying areas where spending can be optimized without compromising on lifestyle quality.

The essence of budgeting lies in its ability to prioritize. Essential needs, debt repayments, and savings should take precedence in any budgeting plan. Savings are particularly crucial, often recommended to be at least 20% of one's income, earmarked for emergencies, retirement, and other long-term financial objectives. This "pay yourself first" approach ensures that savings are not an afterthought but a priority.

Adaptability is a critical feature of effective budgeting. Life is dynamic, marked by unexpected changes, financial windfalls, and unforeseen challenges. A budget, therefore, should not be static but flexible, able to accommodate life's vicissitudes without derailing one's financial goals. Regular reviews and adjustments to the budget ensure it remains relevant and functional, reflecting current financial realities and priorities.

Technology has revolutionized the practice of budgeting, offering tools and apps designed to simplify and enhance the process. These digital aids can track spending in real time, categorize expenses, and even provide insights into spending patterns. The integration of such tools in one's budgeting process can make financial management more accessible and engaging, encouraging consistency and accountability in financial practices.

The psychological benefits of budgeting cannot be overstated. The security and peace of mind afforded by a well-maintained budget contribute significantly to overall well-being. Knowing that finances are under control, with a plan in place to handle emergencies and achieve financial goals, can alleviate stress and anxiety associated with financial uncertainties.

Budgeting also fosters financial discipline, a virtue that extends beyond the realm of money management. The habits cultivated through consistent budgeting—such as delayed gratification, critical assessment of needs versus wants, and goal-oriented saving—can positively influence other areas of life, promoting a more intentional and focused approach to personal and professional endeavors.

In navigating the intricate dance of income, savings, and expenditures, budgeting emerges not just as a tool for financial management but as a blueprint for financial empowerment. It illuminates the path towards fiscal stability, ensuring that every dollar is purposefully spent or saved. Through meticulous planning, regular review, and the integration of modern tools, budgeting transforms the daunting task of financial oversight into a manageable and rewarding journey, steering individuals towards their desired financial destinations.

The Enchantment of Frugal Living

The enchantment of frugal living unfolds in the artful balance of simplicity and abundance, where the judicious use of resources amplifies life's pleasures rather than diminishing them. This lifestyle choice, often misconceived as mere penny-pinching, is in reality a deliberate and thoughtful approach to consumption that champions value, mindfulness, and sustainability over the fleeting allure of material excess. Frugal living invites individuals to a journey of intentional spending, where each decision is infused with a deeper consideration for personal priorities and the collective well-being of the planet.

At the heart of frugal living lies the principle of mindful consumption. This philosophy encourages a reflective pause before each purchase, questioning the necessity, utility, and joy that the item or service will bring. This introspection fosters a deeper appreciation for possessions and experiences, steering individuals away from the impulsive buying that characterizes consumerist cultures. Mindful consumption is not about deprivation but about making more informed, deliberate choices that align with one's values and long-term goals.

The practice of frugality is often accompanied by creative resourcefulness, transforming limitations into a canvas for innovation. Frugal individuals find joy and satisfaction in DIY projects, from home repairs to crafting and gardening, which not only save money but also imbue their lives with a unique personal touch. This creative engagement with the material world fosters a sense of accomplishment and independence, counteracting the passive consumerism that defines modern economies.

Frugal living also champions the ethos of waste reduction, resonating with the urgent call for environmental stewardship in an age of overconsumption and ecological strain. By prioritizing the reuse, repair, and repurposing of items, frugality aligns with sustainable living practices, reducing one's carbon footprint and contributing to a more sustainable global economy. This aspect of frugality is not just an economic choice but a moral stance, reflecting a commitment to living in harmony with the planet.

Moreover, frugal living cultivates financial freedom and security, liberating individuals from the shackles of debt and the perpetual pursuit of more. By living within or below one's means, frugal individuals can allocate more resources toward saving and investing, accelerating the journey towards financial independence. This financial cushion affords them the luxury of choice, be it the choice to pursue a passion, to work less, or to retire early, thus enriching their lives with experiences and engagements that transcend monetary value.

The communal and relational dimensions of frugal living further enrich its appeal. Frugality often fosters a sense of community through the sharing of goods, skills, and time, strengthening social bonds and support networks. This communal aspect is manifest in initiatives like community gardens, tool libraries, and skill-sharing workshops, which not only promote frugality but also engender a sense of belonging and collective resilience.

Frugal living, with its emphasis on simplicity, mindfulness, and sustainability, offers a counter-narrative to the prevailing consumerist ethos that equates happiness with material accumulation. It invites individuals to redefine wealth, not in terms of possessions, but in the quality of their experiences, the depth of their relationships, and the integrity of their engagement with the world. In embracing frugality, one discovers that true abundance lies not in having more but in needing less, finding contentment and joy in the simple, the sustainable, and the meaningful. This lifestyle choice, far from a mere exercise in economization, is a profound journey towards a more intentional, fulfilling, and harmonious existence.

Chapter 8: The Winds of Passive Income

Setting Sail with Investments

Setting sail with investments is akin to embarking on a grand voyage across the vast and often unpredictable ocean of financial markets. It's a journey fraught with both opportunity and risk, requiring a keen sense of navigation, a sturdy vessel built on sound financial principles, and an unwavering commitment to one's long-term financial goals. For those willing to undertake this adventure, the rewards can be substantial, offering not just financial gains but also the invaluable treasure of economic security and independence.

The first step in this investment journey is charting a course, which begins with a clear understanding of one's financial goals and risk tolerance. These goals can range from achieving financial security, funding a child's education, to retiring comfortably. Aligning investment strategies with these objectives is crucial, as it determines the investment horizon, asset allocation, and the level of risk one is willing to assume. Risk tolerance, an intrinsic aspect of any investment strategy, varies widely among individuals and is influenced by factors such as age, income, financial responsibilities, and personal comfort with market volatility.

With goals set and risk tolerance assessed, the next step is assembling the investment vessel, starting with the foundation of a diversified portfolio. Diversification, the strategy of spreading investments across various asset classes such as stocks, bonds, real estate, and commodities, is the keel that keeps the investment ship stable amidst market storms. It mitigates risk by ensuring that the underperformance of one investment can be offset by the gains in another, providing a smoother journey towards financial objectives.

Knowledge and continuous education serve as the compass and charts for navigating the investment seas. The financial landscape is ever-evolving, with new investment vehicles, market dynamics, and economic indicators constantly emerging. Staying informed through reputable financial news sources, educational materials, and professional advice is essential for making informed decisions and adjusting one's investment strategy in response to changing market conditions.

Active portfolio management is the act of steering the investment ship, requiring regular review and rebalancing to ensure alignment with one's investment strategy and risk tolerance. This may involve adjusting asset allocations, taking profits from high-performing investments, or increasing positions in undervalued assets. This proactive approach allows investors to capitalize on market opportunities and guard against potential downturns.

The role of patience and long-term perspective cannot be overstated in the investment journey. The markets are inherently volatile, with periods of significant fluctuations and downturns. A long-term outlook enables investors to weather these storms, avoiding the pitfalls of reactionary selling during downturns or speculative investing during booms. Understanding that wealth accumulation is a gradual process, often spanning decades, fosters the discipline and resilience needed to stay the course and realize one's financial goals.

Risk management is the anchor of any sound investment strategy, safeguarding against potential losses that could capsize one's financial plans. This involves not only diversification and regular portfolio rebalancing but also the strategic use of stop-loss orders, insurance products, and other financial instruments designed to protect against downside risk.

Embarking on the investment journey is a bold and proactive step towards financial autonomy. It requires a blend of strategic planning, ongoing education, disciplined execution, and an unwavering commitment to one's financial aspirations. By setting sail with investments, individuals chart a course towards not just wealth accumulation, but a deeper sense of financial empowerment and the freedom to pursue their life's passions and dreams with confidence.

Real Estate: The Island of Enduring Wealth

Real estate stands as a beacon in the vast ocean of investment opportunities, often heralded as the island of enduring wealth. Its tangible nature, coupled with the potential for both capital appreciation and income generation, makes it a cornerstone in the portfolios of both seasoned investors and novices alike. The allure of real estate investment lies not just in its promise of financial returns but in its capacity to serve as a hedge against inflation and a source of passive income, contributing to a diversified and resilient investment strategy.

The journey into real estate investment begins with an understanding of its multifaceted landscape, which ranges from residential properties and commercial real estate to REITs (Real Estate Investment Trusts) and real estate crowdfunding platforms. Each avenue offers a unique set of opportunities, risks, and considerations, catering to different investment goals, capital outlays, and levels of involvement in property management.

Residential real estate, encompassing single-family homes, apartments, and multifamily units, offers a direct and personal pathway to real estate investment. The appeal of residential properties lies in their dual potential to generate rental income and appreciate in value over time, providing both immediate cash flow and long-term wealth accumulation. Moreover, the emotional gratification of providing homes for individuals and families adds a fulfilling dimension to the investment.

Commercial real estate, which includes office spaces, retail outlets, and industrial properties, presents a different investment profile. Typically involving higher initial investments and longer lease terms, commercial properties can offer stable, long-term rental income streams. However, they also require a deeper understanding of market dynamics, zoning laws, and the economic health of the business sector, underscoring the importance of due diligence and professional advice in commercial real estate ventures.

For those seeking exposure to real estate without the direct ownership responsibilities, REITs offer an accessible and liquid option. These trusts pool investor funds to purchase and manage a portfolio of real estate assets, distributing the majority of income as dividends. Investing in REITs allows individuals to tap into the real estate market with relatively small capital outlay, enjoying the benefits of diversification and professional management.

The digital age has ushered in new frontiers in real estate investment, notably through crowdfunding platforms. These platforms democratize access to real estate ventures, allowing investors to contribute smaller sums towards property investments or development projects. Crowdfunding not only broadens access to real estate deals but also introduces investors to a wider array of projects, from commercial developments to residential renovations.

Despite its attractive prospects, real estate investment is not without its challenges. Market fluctuations, property maintenance, and management responsibilities, and the illiquid nature of direct property investments are factors that demand careful consideration. Successful real estate investing requires a strategic approach, encompassing market research, financial analysis, and an understanding of legal and tax implications.

Moreover, the leverage commonly used in real estate investing can amplify both gains and losses. While mortgage financing can increase the potential return on investment, it also introduces additional risk, emphasizing the need for prudent financial planning and risk management.

Real estate's enduring appeal as an investment lies in its inherent value, the stability of demand for physical space, and its potential to generate wealth across market cycles. Whether through direct property ownership, REITs, or innovative crowdfunding platforms, real estate offers a pathway to financial growth and diversification. It stands as a testament to the timeless adage that investing in land and property is a solid foundation for wealth, offering shelter not just in the physical sense but also in the financial storms that occasionally sweep through the global economy. In navigating the complex yet rewarding landscape of real estate investment, individuals can anchor their financial futures on the solid ground of property, an asset class that has weathered the test of time and market turbulence.

The Digital Age: Online Ventures and Passive Streams

The digital age has unfurled a vast expanse of opportunities, revolutionizing how we perceive, create, and accumulate wealth. Online ventures and passive income streams, once the outliers of the investment world, have now taken center stage, offering innovative pathways to financial independence. This transformation is underpinned by the internet's ubiquity, which has democratized access to markets, resources, and audiences on an unprecedented scale. In this new era, the barriers to entry for entrepreneurship and investment have been dramatically lowered, making the dream of generating sustained income more accessible to a broader swath of society.

Online ventures, in their myriad forms, from e-commerce platforms and digital marketplaces to content creation and affiliate marketing, present a fertile ground for entrepreneurial endeavors. E-commerce platforms, for instance, allow individuals to set up virtual storefronts with minimal overhead, selling products to a global audience. The scalability of such ventures is immense, with the potential to transition from side hustles to full-fledged businesses.

Similarly, content creation, through blogs, videos, or podcasts, offers a platform for individuals to monetize their expertise, interests, or creativity. The digital ecosystem supports these endeavors with tools and platforms that facilitate content distribution and monetization, such as advertising revenue, sponsored content, and subscription models. These avenues not only provide financial returns but also the satisfaction of building engaged communities around shared interests or knowledge.

Affiliate marketing represents another facet of online ventures, where individuals can earn commissions by promoting products or services through their digital channels. This performance-based model rewards the ability to influence and engage audiences, leveraging trust and credibility to generate sales for partner businesses.

Beyond active online ventures, the digital age has also expanded the avenues for generating passive income, where the initial effort is followed by sustained revenue with minimal ongoing work. Digital products, such as e-books, courses, and software, exemplify this model. Once created, these products can be sold repeatedly without the need for inventory or significant additional effort, providing a continuous income stream.

Investment platforms have also been transformed by the digital revolution. Fintech innovations have given rise to robo-advisors, online investment platforms, and peer-to-peer lending, making financial markets and investment opportunities more accessible. These platforms offer automated, algorithm-driven financial planning services with minimal human supervision, lowering the cost and complexity of investing, and enabling individuals to build diversified portfolios that can generate passive income through dividends, interest, and capital gains.

Real estate crowdfunding is another testament to the digital age's impact on passive income opportunities. By pooling resources with other investors online, individuals can participate in real estate investments with smaller capital, enjoying the benefits of property ownership, including rental income and property appreciation, without the burdens of direct management.

The allure of online ventures and passive income streams lies not only in their financial potential but also in the flexibility and autonomy they offer. They embody the quintessential aspiration of the digital age: to live and work on one's own terms, free from the constraints of traditional employment and geographical boundaries. This freedom, however, comes with the need for digital literacy, adaptability, and a proactive approach to learning and personal development.

Moreover, the digital landscape is inherently dynamic, with rapid technological advancements and shifting market trends. Success in this realm requires a commitment to continuous education, staying abreast of digital trends, and the agility to pivot strategies in response to evolving opportunities and challenges.

In navigating the digital age's vast potential for online ventures and passive income streams, individuals are empowered to chart their unique paths toward financial independence. This era, characterized by its digital infrastructure, offers an unprecedented platform for innovation, entrepreneurship, and wealth creation, redefining the paradigms of work, income, and success.

Examples for Online Ventures and Passive Income Streams

E-commerce Stores: Platforms like Shopify and Etsy have made it easier for individuals to open online stores selling everything from handmade crafts to drop-shipped products.

Digital Content Creation: YouTubers, bloggers, and podcasters monetize their content through advertising, sponsorships, and subscriber donations on platforms like YouTube, WordPress, and Patreon.

Freelancing and Consulting: Websites like Upwork and Fiverr provide a marketplace for professionals to offer their services in writing, graphic design, web development, and more, to a global client base.

Online Courses and E-books: Platforms such as Udemy and Amazon Kindle Direct Publishing allow experts in various fields to create and sell courses and e-books.

Affiliate Marketing: Individuals can create niche websites or blogs that generate income through affiliate links to products and services, earning a commission for each sale made through their referral.

Mobile App Development: Developers can create and monetize apps through in-app purchases, advertising, or premium app sales on platforms like the Apple App Store or Google Play.

Passive Income Streams

Stock Photography: Photographers can upload their work to stock photography websites like Shutterstock or Getty Images, earning royalties each time their photos are downloaded.

Royalties from Creative Works: Musicians, authors, and artists can earn royalties from their work through platforms like Spotify for music, or royalties from book sales on Amazon.

Investment Dividends: Investing in dividend-yielding stocks or ETFs through online brokerage platforms can provide a steady stream of passive income.

Peer-to-Peer (P2P) Lending: Platforms like LendingClub allow individuals to lend money to others in exchange for interest payments, creating a passive income stream.

Real Estate Crowdfunding: Websites like Fundrise or RealtyMogul enable individuals to invest in real estate projects with relatively small amounts of money, earning a share of the rental income or profits from property sales.

Automated Blogs or Websites: Creating a content-rich website that's optimized for search engine traffic can generate passive income through advertising and affiliate marketing, with minimal ongoing effort after the initial setup.

Online Marketplaces: Setting up a shop on an online marketplace like Etsy for handmade goods, or Tindie for electronics, where products can be sold repeatedly without constant supervision.

Chapter 9: The Lighthouse of Legacy

Protecting Your Wealth with Insurance and Wills

Protecting your wealth with insurance and wills is an essential aspect of comprehensive financial planning, safeguarding not just the financial assets you've accumulated over a lifetime but also ensuring the well-being of your loved ones in your absence. This dual strategy acts as a bulwark against unforeseen calamities and the complexities of estate distribution, ensuring that your legacy is preserved and passed on according to your wishes.

Insurance, in its myriad forms, serves as a critical tool in the wealth protection arsenal. Life insurance, for instance, provides financial security to your dependents, offering a safety net in the event of an untimely demise. It ensures that financial obligations, such as mortgages, education costs, and day-to-day living expenses, can be met, preserving the standard of living you've worked hard to establish for your family. Beyond life insurance, other forms, such as disability and long-term care insurance, protect against the financial drain associated with long-term illness or incapacitation, safeguarding your assets from being depleted by healthcare costs.

Property and casualty insurance further extend the protective shield around your wealth. Homeowners' insurance protects against losses to your primary residence, one of the most significant investments most people make. Similarly, auto and liability insurance safeguard against the financial repercussions of accidents and lawsuits, which can erode wealth rapidly without adequate coverage. In essence, these insurance policies act as a financial defense mechanism, mitigating the risks that can lead to significant financial loss.

On the other hand, wills serve as a navigational chart for your estate posthumously, ensuring that your assets are distributed according to your wishes. A well-crafted will is the cornerstone of an effective estate plan, delineating the beneficiaries of your assets, the guardians for minor children, and the executors who will oversee the estate's distribution. Without a will, the distribution of your estate is left to the state's intestacy laws, which may not align with your personal wishes, leading to potential familial discord and legal complications.

Beyond the basic will, estate planning can involve more complex instruments like trusts, which offer greater control over the distribution of your assets. Trusts can minimize estate taxes, protect assets from creditors, and stipulate conditions under which beneficiaries can access their inheritance, ensuring that your wealth serves the purposes you intend, even in your absence.

The importance of regular reviews and updates to insurance policies and wills cannot be overstated. Life's milestones—marriage, the birth of children, significant acquisitions, and changes in financial status—necessitate adjustments to these documents to reflect your current situation and priorities. Regular reviews ensure that your coverage remains adequate and your estate plan aligns with your evolving wishes and circumstances.

Moreover, the integration of insurance and estate planning within a broader financial strategy ensures a holistic approach to wealth management. Coordination with financial advisors, estate planning attorneys, and insurance agents is crucial to align these components with your overall financial goals, optimizing protection and minimizing potential gaps in coverage or planning.

In navigating the complexities of wealth protection, education and professional advice are invaluable. Understanding the nuances of different insurance products, the implications of estate planning decisions, and the legal and tax ramifications of various strategies empowers individuals to make informed choices. Professional advisors can offer tailored recommendations, ensuring that your wealth protection strategy is robust, comprehensive, and aligned with your unique circumstances and objectives.

Protecting your wealth with insurance and wills is not merely a transactional task but a fundamental aspect of stewarding your financial legacy. It's about ensuring that the wealth you've worked tirelessly to build serves not just your lifetime goals but also provides for your loved ones in the future. Through careful planning, regular review, and professional guidance, you can secure your financial legacy, providing peace of mind that your wealth is shielded against life's uncertainties and poised for a purposeful transition to future generations.

Philanthropy: Sharing Your Treasure

Philanthropy, the act of sharing one's treasure to make a positive impact on society, transcends mere financial contributions to embody a broader commitment to the welfare of humanity. It represents a profound expression of empathy, compassion, and responsibility, where individuals leverage their wealth, resources, and influence to address societal challenges, foster equality, and promote sustainable development. This noble pursuit not only enriches the lives of beneficiaries but also imbues the donor's life with a deeper sense of purpose and fulfillment.

At the heart of effective philanthropy lies strategic giving, which goes beyond spontaneous donations to encompass a thoughtful, informed approach to charitable contributions. Strategic philanthropists seek to understand the root causes of societal issues, identifying areas where their contributions can have the most significant, enduring impact. This might involve supporting education initiatives to empower future generations, funding healthcare research to combat diseases, or investing in sustainable development projects to address environmental challenges. By focusing on systemic change, strategic philanthropy aims to create lasting solutions rather than temporary relief.

The democratization of philanthropy in the digital age has broadened the scope of potential donors, moving beyond the realm of the ultra-wealthy to include individuals from various economic backgrounds. Crowdfunding platforms, social media campaigns, and donor-advised funds have made it easier for everyday philanthropists to contribute to causes they are passionate about, regardless of the donation size. This inclusivity has expanded the philanthropic landscape, fostering a collective approach to problem-solving and community building.

Corporate philanthropy and social responsibility initiatives further illustrate the multifaceted nature of modern philanthropy. Businesses, recognizing their role in society, are increasingly integrating philanthropic efforts into their core operations. This shift towards corporate social responsibility (CSR) not only addresses societal issues but also aligns with the values of customers, employees, and stakeholders, creating a symbiotic relationship between business success and social progress.

In addition to financial contributions, philanthropy also encompasses the sharing of time, expertise, and resources. Volunteerism, mentorship programs, and the provision of pro bono services are vital components of a holistic philanthropic strategy. These non-monetary contributions harness the unique skills and experiences of individuals to make a direct, tangible impact on communities and causes.

The benefits of philanthropy extend beyond the immediate recipients of generosity. Donors often experience a profound sense of satisfaction and happiness from giving, a phenomenon supported by numerous psychological studies. This emotional reward, known as the "helper's high," reinforces the intrinsic value of generosity, fostering a virtuous cycle of giving and well-being.

Philanthropy also plays a crucial role in legacy building, allowing individuals to imprint their values and vision on the world. Through foundations, endowments, and charitable trusts, philanthropists can ensure that their commitment to societal betterment endures beyond their lifetime, inspiring future generations to continue the legacy of giving.

Transparency and accountability are critical in maintaining the integrity of philanthropic endeavors. Donors increasingly seek assurance that their contributions are being used effectively, prompting charitable organizations to adopt higher standards of transparency and impact measurement. This accountability not only builds trust between donors and organizations but also enhances the efficacy of philanthropic projects, ensuring that resources are directed where they are most needed.

In navigating the landscape of philanthropy, collaboration and partnership stand out as key strategies for amplifying impact. By joining forces with other donors, non-profits, governments, and the private sector, philanthropists can leverage collective resources and expertise to tackle complex, multifaceted issues. These collaborative efforts underscore the interconnectedness of societal challenges and the need for unified action to achieve meaningful change.

Philanthropy, in its essence, is a testament to the power of shared humanity and collective action. It embodies the belief that through generosity, collaboration, and strategic intervention, individuals can contribute to a more equitable, just, and sustainable world. In sharing one's treasure, be it wealth, time, or expertise, philanthropy offers a pathway to not only transform the lives of others but also to enrich one's own life with purpose and connection.

Building a Legacy that Lasts

Building a legacy that lasts transcends the accumulation of wealth or achievements to encompass the enduring impact one has on the world, their community, and future generations. It is about crafting a narrative of one's life that continues to resonate and influence long after they have passed, through thoughtful actions, contributions to society, and the values instilled in others. This concept of legacy is deeply intertwined with the notions of purpose, meaning, and the desire to leave the world a better place than one found it.

At the foundation of a lasting legacy lies the clarity of values and principles. These core beliefs act as the guiding stars in life's journey, influencing decisions, actions, and the paths one chooses to pursue. Whether it's integrity, compassion, innovation, or leadership, these values become the threads woven into the fabric of one's legacy, reflected in every endeavor and interaction.

The pursuit of impactful achievements is often a significant component of legacy building. This might manifest in various forms, such as groundbreaking contributions to a field of work, the establishment of successful enterprises that create jobs and drive economic growth, or significant philanthropic efforts that address societal challenges. However, achievements alone do not define a legacy; it is the motivation behind these accomplishments and their alignment with one's values that imbue them with lasting significance.

Mentorship and the transfer of knowledge play a pivotal role in legacy building. By sharing wisdom, experiences, and lessons learned with others, individuals can extend their influence far beyond their personal reach, shaping the minds and futures of protégés, colleagues, and even strangers. This act of passing the torch not only enriches the lives of recipients but also ensures that one's insights and values continue to inspire and guide long after they are gone.

Family and community are central to the notion of a lasting legacy. The traditions, values, and culture shared within a family, and the contributions made to one's community, create a tangible and enduring legacy that transcends material wealth. This might involve nurturing a loving, supportive family environment, contributing to community development, or engaging in acts of service that reinforce communal bonds and collective well-being.

Philanthropy, as an extension of one's values and commitment to societal betterment, is a powerful vehicle for legacy building. Through charitable giving, the establishment of foundations, or active involvement in causes close to one's heart, individuals can effect positive change that resonates across generations. This philanthropic spirit, rooted in empathy and a sense of shared humanity, becomes a hallmark of one's legacy, reflecting a life dedicated to the upliftment of others.

The documentation of one's life story, philosophies, and experiences, whether through memoirs, oral histories, or digital media, serves as a repository of wisdom for future generations. This act of storytelling not only preserves the individual's journey and insights but also offers guidance, inspiration, and a sense of connection to those who follow.

In crafting a legacy, the focus on sustainable and ethical practices ensures that one's impact is not only positive but also enduring. This involves considering the long-term implications of one's actions on the environment, society, and future generations, striving for a balance between progress and sustainability.

Building a legacy that lasts is a deliberate and intentional endeavor, requiring reflection, action, and a commitment to living one's values. It is about making a difference in the lives of others, contributing to the greater good, and leaving a mark that continues to inspire, guide, and influence long after one's time has passed. In this pursuit, the true measure of a legacy is not found in the wealth or accolades amassed but in the positive impact on the world and the lives touched along the way.

Chapter 10: The Treasure Island

Arriving at Your Financial Destination

Arriving at your financial destination is akin to reaching the summit of a meticulously planned expedition, a journey marked by strategic decisions, disciplined saving, and astute investing. It's the culmination of years, often decades, of dedicated effort towards achieving a state of financial security and independence where one's financial goals are not just aspirations but realities.

The journey begins with the establishment of clear, measurable financial goals. These objectives act as the North Star, guiding financial decisions and actions. Whether it's achieving debt freedom, owning a home, securing a comfortable retirement, or leaving a substantial legacy, these goals provide direction and purpose to one's financial journey.

A comprehensive financial plan serves as the roadmap to this destination. Tailored to individual goals, circumstances, and risk tolerance, this plan outlines the strategies for saving, investing, and managing debt. It incorporates milestones to mark progress and contingencies to address the inevitable uncertainties of life. Regular reviews and adjustments ensure the plan remains aligned with changing life stages, financial situations, and goals.

Disciplined saving is the fuel that propels one towards their financial destination. It involves living within or below one's means, prioritizing savings, and making conscious spending decisions. Automating savings can streamline this process, ensuring a portion of every income is directed towards savings or investment accounts before it can be spent elsewhere.

Investing wisely accelerates the journey, harnessing the power of compound interest and market growth to grow wealth. Diversification across asset classes, sectors, and geographies mitigates risk and enhances the potential for returns. Staying informed, seeking professional advice, and maintaining a long-term perspective can navigate the volatility of markets and capitalize on investment opportunities.

Debt management is crucial in avoiding detours and setbacks. High-interest debt, particularly from credit cards or personal loans, can severely impede financial progress. Strategies such as debt consolidation, the snowball or avalanche methods, and renegotiation of loan terms can help manage and eventually eliminate debt, freeing up more resources for saving and investing.

Risk management through insurance safeguards the journey against unforeseen events. Life, health, disability, and property insurance protect against significant financial losses due to accidents, illness, or other calamities, ensuring that unexpected events don't derail one's financial plans.

Financial literacy is the compass that ensures one stays on course. Understanding financial principles, products, and markets empowers individuals to make informed decisions, avoid pitfalls, and seize opportunities. Continuous learning, through reading, courses, and consultation with financial advisors, keeps one's knowledge current and applicable.

Patience and perseverance are the virtues that underpin success in reaching one's financial destination. The journey is often long and fraught with challenges, requiring resilience to stay the course and adapt to changing circumstances. Celebrating milestones along the way can provide motivation and reinforce the commitment to achieving one's financial goals.

Arriving at your financial destination brings a profound sense of accomplishment and peace of mind. It's the realization of financial freedom, where work becomes a choice rather than a necessity, and life can be lived on one's own terms. This financial nirvana allows for greater focus on passions, hobbies, and philanthropy, enriching one's life and the lives of others.

In summary, arriving at your financial destination is the result of a deliberate and disciplined approach to personal finance, encompassing goal setting, planning, saving, investing, and risk management. It's a journey that demands patience, resilience, and continuous learning, but the reward is a state of financial security and independence that provides a foundation for a fulfilling life.

The Ritual of Regular Financial Review

The ritual of regular financial review is a critical discipline in the stewardship of one's financial health, akin to the periodic maintenance required to keep a well-oiled machine running smoothly. This systematic examination of one's financial standing and progress towards goals is not merely an administrative task but a strategic exercise that ensures alignment with broader financial objectives and readiness to adapt to life's ever-changing dynamics.

At its core, a regular financial review involves a detailed analysis of income, expenses, savings, investments, debts, and insurance coverage. This comprehensive appraisal provides a panoramic view of one's financial landscape, highlighting strengths, uncovering vulnerabilities, and identifying opportunities for optimization.

Income review is the starting point, where one assesses the stability, sufficiency, and growth prospects of their earnings. This evaluation may lead to strategies for income diversification, negotiation for raises, or pursuits of additional revenue streams, ensuring that the foundation of one's financial structure remains robust and capable of supporting future aspirations.

Expenses come under scrutiny next, with a focus on identifying and eliminating wasteful spending, optimizing costs, and reallocating funds towards higher priority areas such as debt repayment or savings. This exercise often reveals surprising insights into spending patterns, prompting more mindful consumption and greater financial discipline.

Savings and investments warrant a significant portion of the review, assessing not just the amounts saved and returns generated but also the alignment with one's risk tolerance and investment horizon. This segment may involve rebalancing investment portfolios, adjusting savings rates, or revising investment strategies to reflect changes in market conditions, personal circumstances, or financial goals.

Debt analysis is another crucial element, where existing liabilities are examined for interest rates, repayment terms, and overall impact on financial health. This may lead to strategies for debt consolidation, refinancing to more favorable terms, or accelerated repayment plans to reduce the interest burden and clear the path towards financial freedom.

Insurance coverage, often overlooked, is a vital component of the financial review process. It involves ensuring that policies remain adequate to protect against life's uncertainties and that beneficiaries, coverage amounts, and policy terms are up-to-date. This reassessment may lead to adjustments in coverage to guard against emerging risks or to optimize insurance costs.

Beyond these pillars, the financial review also encompasses estate planning elements such as wills, trusts, and healthcare directives, ensuring that these critical documents reflect current wishes and legal requirements. This ensures that one's legacy and intentions are preserved and that loved ones are provided for according to one's wishes.

The frequency of these reviews can vary, but a semi-annual or annual rhythm is commonly recommended. However, significant life events such as marriage, the birth of a child, career changes, or substantial shifts in financial circumstances warrant immediate reviews to adjust one's financial plan accordingly.

Technology plays a pivotal role in facilitating regular financial reviews, with a plethora of tools and apps available to track finances, investments, and budgets in real-time. These digital aids not only streamline the review process but also provide actionable insights and alerts, making it easier to stay on top of one's financial game.

The ritual of regular financial review embodies a proactive approach to personal finance, fostering a deep understanding of one's financial situation and facilitating informed decision-making. It's a process that not only safeguards against potential financial pitfalls but also paves the way for wealth accumulation, risk management, and the achievement of long-term financial aspirations. By institutionalizing this ritual, individuals can navigate the complexities of personal finance with confidence, ensuring that their financial ship remains steadfastly on course towards their desired future.

The Never-ending Journey of Wealth and Personal Growth

The pursuit of wealth and personal growth is a never-ending journey, an odyssey that transcends the mere accumulation of financial assets to encompass a holistic development of the self. This voyage is not linear but a dynamic interplay of advancements and setbacks, learning and unlearning, striving and reflecting. It is about cultivating a mindset that views wealth not just as an end goal but as a means to broader life objectives, including personal fulfillment, empowerment, and the ability to make a positive impact on the world.

At the heart of this journey is the concept of continuous personal development, the commitment to self-improvement and the acquisition of knowledge. This encompasses not only financial literacy, understanding the mechanisms of wealth creation, investment, and management, but also the broader aspects of personal growth such as emotional intelligence, resilience, and leadership. The pursuit of knowledge is unending, with each new insight laying the groundwork for more informed decisions, both in finance and in life.

The integration of wealth creation with personal values and ethics marks a significant milestone on this journey. It involves aligning financial goals with personal beliefs and priorities, ensuring that the quest for wealth does not compromise one's integrity or sense of purpose. This alignment brings about a sense of coherence and authenticity, where financial decisions reflect and reinforce one's identity and values.

Wealth, in the context of this journey, is not solely defined by monetary measures but also by the richness of one's experiences, relationships, and contributions to society. It encompasses the ability to live life on one's own terms, with the freedom and resources to pursue passions, support loved ones, and give back to the community. This broader perspective on wealth elevates the pursuit from a self-centered endeavor to a more inclusive, purpose-driven quest.

Personal growth within this journey also entails developing a robust mental and emotional framework to navigate the vicissitudes of life and wealth. It is about building resilience to withstand financial downturns and personal challenges, cultivating a mindset of abundance that focuses on opportunities rather than constraints, and fostering gratitude and contentment with one's achievements.

The concept of legacy is deeply intertwined with the never-ending journey of wealth and personal growth. It's about the imprint one leaves on the world, the positive changes enacted, and the lives touched. Building a legacy involves not only the transfer of wealth to future generations but also the passing down of values, wisdom, and a spirit of generosity. This legacy becomes a beacon for others, inspiring and guiding them on their own journeys.

The role of mentorship and community in this journey cannot be overstated. Surrounding oneself with like-minded individuals, mentors who have navigated similar paths, and a community that supports and challenges one to grow, can exponentially enhance the journey. These relationships provide guidance, inspiration, and a sense of belonging, reinforcing the commitment to continuous growth and wealth creation.

The journey of wealth and personal growth is also marked by the willingness to adapt and pivot. In an ever-changing world, the ability to evolve one's strategies, goals, and even values in response to new information, experiences, and insights is crucial. This adaptability ensures that one remains relevant, fulfilled, and aligned with their evolving definition of success.

In summary, the never-ending journey of wealth and personal growth is a multifaceted voyage that transcends financial prosperity to encompass a holistic development of the self. It is a journey marked by continuous learning, ethical wealth creation, resilience, and the pursuit of a meaningful legacy. Through this journey, wealth becomes not just an end but a means to a richer, more fulfilling life, woven with personal achievements, contributions to society, and the continuous evolution of the self.

Conclusion

As we draw the curtains on this journey, it's evident that the voyage of wealth and personal growth is continuous, with no final destination but rather a path of endless discovery and evolution. This book has endeavored to equip you with the tools, insights, and perspectives necessary to navigate this journey with purpose and grace.

The intertwining of financial wisdom with personal development principles presented herein serves as a testament to the belief that true wealth is not merely about financial accumulation but about living a life that resonates with your deepest values and aspirations. It's about making choices that not only secure your financial future but also enrich your life and the lives of those around you.

As you move forward, let the principles and strategies explored become your compass, guiding your decisions and actions. Remember, the journey of wealth and personal growth is uniquely yours—shaped by your dreams, values, and the legacy you wish to create.

May this book serve as a beacon, illuminating your path toward a life of abundance, purpose, and fulfillment. Embrace the journey, for it is in the pursuit of wealth and personal growth that life's true riches are found.

RESOURCES

I

Below is a resource guide that includes books, websites, podcasts, and courses that delve deeper into key themes such as financial literacy, investment strategies, mindfulness, and life coaching. These resources are to complement the concepts discussed and provide further learning opportunities.

Books on Financial Literacy and Investment Strategies:

- "The Total Money Makeover" by Dave Ramsey offers a straightforward plan for achieving financial health, focusing on debt elimination and savings.

- "Rich Dad Poor Dad" by Robert Kiyosaki explores the differences in mindset between the author's two "dads" and their approaches to money and investing.

- "The 7 Habits of Highly Effective People" by Stephen R. Covey provides insights into personal effectiveness and leadership.

- "Atomic Habits" by James Clear delves into the power of small habits in making significant life changes.

- "Thinking, Fast and Slow" by Daniel Kahneman, a Nobel laureate, examines the ways in which the human mind makes decisions, including financial ones.

Websites

- Investopedia (https://www.investopedia.com) offers a wealth of information on financial topics, from basic concepts to advanced investment strategies.

- The Financial Diet (https://thefinancialdiet.com) provides relatable financial advice for young adults, covering budgeting, saving, and investing.

- Mr. Money Mustache (https://www.mrmoneymustache.com) shares insights on frugal living and achieving financial independence early in life.

- Maconomics (https://maconomics.com) Ross Mac provides financial education as a former Wall Street professional.

Podcasts

- "The Dave Ramsey Show" offers practical advice on debt elimination, budgeting, and building wealth.

- "How I Built This" by Guy Raz (NPR) shares stories behind some of the world's best-known companies, offering insights into entrepreneurship and success.

- "Afford Anything" by Paula Pant focuses on making smart decisions about money, time, and life to align daily behaviors with life's overarching goals.

Online Courses

- "Financial Markets" by Yale University on Coursera (https://www.coursera.org/learn/financial-markets-global) provides an overview of financial markets, including smart investment strategies and risk management.

- "Personal & Family Financial Planning" by University of Florida on Coursera (https://www.coursera.org/learn/family-planning) covers practical financial planning advice for households.

- "Investing In Real Estate" by Udemy (https://www.udemy.com/course/real-estate-investing/) offers insights into various aspects of real estate investment, from property analysis to financing options.

Each resource has been chosen for its ability to offer valuable insights, practical advice, and diverse perspectives on achieving financial well-being and personal growth.

Reflection Prompts for Financial and Personal Growth:

Understanding Your Financial Values:

1. What are my core values when it comes to money and wealth?

2. How do these values influence my spending, saving, and investment decisions?

3. In what ways can I better align my financial decisions with my core values?

Setting and Evaluating Financial Goals:

1. What are my short-term, mid-term, and long-term financial goals?

2. How do these goals reflect what's truly important to me in life?

3. What progress have I made towards these goals, and what challenges have I encountered?

Mindful Spending:

1. What was my most meaningful purchase in the past month, and why?

2. Are there any recurring expenses that don't bring me joy or value? How can I adjust them?

3. How does my spending align with my financial goals and values?

Savings and Investment Reflection:

1. How do I feel about my current savings and investment strategy?

2. What fears or challenges do I face when thinking about saving or investing more?

3. How can I educate myself further to make more informed investment decisions?

Debt Management:

1. What emotions do I associate with my current debt situation?

2. How has debt impacted my financial and personal life?

3. What steps can I take to manage or reduce my debt more effectively?

Income Streams and Career:

1. Am I satisfied with my current income streams? If not, what changes would I like to make?

2. How does my career align with my personal values and financial goals?

3. What opportunities can I explore to increase my income in a way that feels fulfilling and sustainable?

Insurance and Risk Management:

1. Do I feel adequately protected by my current insurance policies?

2. What potential financial risks am I most concerned about, and how can I mitigate them?

3. How regularly do I review my insurance needs, and what prompts these reviews?

Philanthropy and Giving Back:

1. What causes are most important to me, and how do I support them?

2. How does giving back fit into my financial plan and personal values?

3. What more can I do to contribute to the causes I care about, both financially and non-financially?

Legacy and Estate Planning:

1. What do I want my financial legacy to look like?

2. Have I taken the necessary steps to ensure my assets are distributed according to my wishes?

3. How can I involve my family in discussions about estate planning and legacy building?

Online Platforms for Financial Interactive Learning:

1. **Khan Academy (Personal Finance)**:

   - **Website**: khanacademy.org

   - **Description**: Offers a comprehensive range of free courses on personal finance, including savings, investing, mortgages, and retirement planning, complete with interactive exercises and videos.

2. **Udemy**:

   - **Website**: udemy.com

   - **Description**: Features a wide array of courses on financial topics, from basic personal finance and budgeting to advanced investment strategies and financial modeling, taught by industry experts.

3. **Coursera (Financial Planning & Management Courses)**:

   - **Website**: coursera.org

   - **Description**: Provides access to courses and specializations from universities and colleges on financial management, investment, and financial planning, often with interactive quizzes and peer-reviewed assignments.

4. **edX (Finance Courses)**:

   - **Website**: edx.org

   - **Description**: Offers finance courses from top universities around the world, covering topics such as financial analysis, risk management, and behavioral finance.

Community Forums for Financial Discussions:

1. **Reddit (r/personalfinance, r/investing, r/FinancialIndependence)**:

   - **Website**: reddit.com

   - **Description**: Reddit hosts a variety of finance-related communities where users can ask questions, share experiences, and discuss topics ranging from basic budgeting to complex investment strategies.

2. **Bogleheads**:

   - **Website**: bogleheads.org

   - **Description**: A community focused on investment advice inspired by Jack Bogle, the founder of Vanguard. It's a great resource for discussions on index fund investing, personal finance, and retirement planning.

3. **Stack Exchange (Personal Finance & Money)**:

   - **Website**: money.stackexchange.com

   - **Description**: A Q&A platform where users can ask and answer questions on a wide range of financial topics, including personal finance, investments, and tax planning.

4. **The Motley Fool Community Forums**:

   - **Website**: fool.com

   - **Description**: Offers discussion boards on various financial topics, including stock analysis, investment strategies, and personal finance tips, with a focus on long-term, value-oriented investing.

Whether you're a beginner seeking foundational knowledge or an experienced investor looking to refine your strategy, these resources can offer support and guidance on your financial journey.

Global Perspectives Section

In today's interconnected world, understanding the global landscape of finance and wealth management is more crucial than ever. This section delves into how different cultures approach wealth accumulation, investment, saving habits, and personal growth, offering readers a broader view of financial practices and philosophies across the globe.

1. **Savings and Investment Cultures**:

   - **East Asia (China, Japan, South Korea)**: Known for high savings rates, these cultures emphasize financial prudence and long-term planning, with a strong preference for real estate and conservative investment vehicles.

   - **Nordic Countries (Sweden, Norway, Denmark)**: With comprehensive social welfare systems, there's a notable balance between saving for personal goals and relying on state-provided security, leading to a unique approach to personal finance and risk-taking.

2. **Approaches to Debt and Credit**:

   - **United States**: Credit is widely used and accessible, with credit scores playing a significant role in financial health. There's a cultural acceptance of debt as a tool for building wealth, particularly through mortgages and student loans.

   - **Middle East (Saudi Arabia, UAE)**: Islamic finance principles, which prohibit interest (riba), shape approaches to debt and credit, leading to unique financial products that comply with Sharia law.

3. **Philanthropy and Community Support**:

   - **Sub-Saharan Africa**: The concept of "Ubuntu," meaning "I am because we are," reflects a strong tradition of community support and informal giving, which plays a crucial role in social welfare and community development.

- **United States and Europe**: Formal philanthropy is widespread, with established charitable organizations and tax-incentive structures. There's also a growing trend towards impact investing, where investments are made with the intention to generate social and environmental impact alongside a financial return.

4. **Retirement and Social Security Systems**:

- **Latin America (Chile, Brazil)**: These countries have undergone significant pension reforms, transitioning from state-run to privatized systems, affecting how individuals plan and save for retirement.

- **Europe (Germany, France)**: With aging populations and generous state pension systems, there's an ongoing debate about the sustainability of these systems and the need for individual retirement savings.

5. **Cultural Attitudes Towards Wealth and Success**:

- **India**: Success is often measured by one's contribution to family and community well-being, alongside personal achievements. There's a growing interest in entrepreneurship as a means to wealth creation.

- **Scandinavian Countries**: The "Law of Jante" reflects a cultural preference for equality and collective success over individual wealth accumulation, influencing attitudes towards wealth display and consumption.

6. **Financial Education and Literacy Initiatives**:

- **Australia**: The "National Financial Literacy Strategy" is a government initiative aimed at improving financial literacy across all demographics, emphasizing the importance of education in achieving financial well-being.

- **Singapore**: Known for its high level of financial literacy, Singapore integrates financial education into the national curriculum from a young age, preparing individuals to make informed financial decisions.

This global perspective section underscores the diversity in financial practices and philosophies across the world, shaped by cultural norms, economic systems, and societal values. By exploring these varied approaches, readers can gain insights into alternative strategies for wealth accumulation, risk management, and personal growth, enriching their understanding of global finance and fostering a more holistic view of personal financial management.